GREEN WASHED

GREEN WASHED

WHY WE CAN'T BUY OUR WAY TO A GREEN PLANET

KENDRA PIERRE-LOUIS

PUBLISHING
BROOKLYN, NEW YORK

Printed in the United States of America
10 9 8 7 6 5 4 3 2 1

Ig Publishing
392 Clinton Avenue
Brooklyn, NY 11238
www.igpub.com

Library of Congress Cataloging-in-Publication Data

Pierre-Louis, Kendra.
Green washed : why we can't buy our way to a green planet / by Kendra Pierre-Louis.
p. cm.
Includes bibliographical references.
ISBN 978-1-935439-43-1
1. Sustainable living--Economic aspects. 2. Environmentalism--Economic aspects. I. Title.
GE196.P54 2012
338.9'27--dc23

2011053279

A truly good book teaches me better than to read it. I must soon lay it down and commence living on its hint. What I began by reading, I must finish by acting.

—Henry David Thoreau

Consumption, from the Latin word consumptiō meaning a wasting.

CONTENTS

PREFACE

As I was getting gas for my car one day, it dawned on me that I no longer felt comfortable giving any of the oil companies my hard earned money in exchange for their gas. None of my choices—whether it be the company that had caused the third largest oil spill in American history (Exxon-Mobil), the company that had precipitated one of the largest oil spills in world history (BP), or the company that had been implicated in the murder of indigenous protestors fighting for their way of life (Shell)—seemed particularly desirable. However, if I still wanted to drive a car, I had no choice but to buy gas.

From experience, I have found that most people deal with these types of "no-win" choices in one of two ways. On the one hand, many people choose simply not to worry about their choices at all. They feel that, ultimately, there's nothing they can do to change the situation. I call this the "ostrich approach" based on the commonly held belief that when an ostrich senses danger, it will stick its head in the ground. Those who tend towards this way of thinking believe that if they are able to ignore the existence of something unpleasant, it can't hurt them. The problem with this approach, however, is that ostriches don't actually stick their heads in the ground. In reality, when an ostrich senses danger, it lowers its head to the ground to better blend in with the surrounding environment. Ostriches actually do see the danger in front of them, and react in a way that doesn't ignore the problem, but rather protects them from it.

The other common response to no-win choices is to avoid purchasing anything except those products that have been properly vetted and labeled as environmentally and ethically acceptable. I call this the "Atlas method," as people who engage in this type of behavior have a tendency to feel as though they're carrying the weight of the world on their shoulders. Needless to say, this method is not only exhausting, but it can also leave you paralyzed in the egg aisle of your local supermarket, incapable of choosing between eggs from chickens raised in a humane and sustainable manner but which have been placed in a plastic container, or eggs from conventionally raised chickens that are in a completely biodegradable carton (Not that I speak from experience).

Ultimately, these different approaches are not really about eggs, or gas. The real issue is why we even have to purchase gasoline in the first place, or why we have to make buying eggs a Sisyphean task when it's possible to have gloriously, richly yolked eggs raised in a sustainable manner that aren't housed in a container that kills marine life. Instead of spending all of our time avoiding the Witch and begging to see the Wizard, why aren't we instead questioning the underlying structure of Oz?

The idea for this book came about from this very question. I wanted to stop looking at "stuff" in isolation and instead start examining the systems and structures that exist behind that stuff. An increasingly rich body of economic, ecologic, and psychological research supports the supposition woven throughout this book that if we want to bring our planet and the people who inhabit it to a healthy place, we have to reevaluate our relationship with "stuff" and with each other in a way that's far more significant than purchasing an organic granola bar instead of a conventional one, or buying eco-friendly sex toys (they do exist). While I personally make a concerted effort to engage in behaviors that I know are more sustainable, I don't in believe that by getting my produce from a local CSA (Community Supported Agriculture) instead of from the supermarket, I've engaged in a transformative act. Sure it's better, for me, for the environment, and for the farm where I purchase my produce, but it's not transformative because it's still an individual act within a larger unsustainable system.

The reason I have chosen to specifically focus on green products is because while everyone already knows that oil is bad for the environment and that plastic bags choke sea turtles, we seem to have faltered in our understanding of how we got to a place in our collective culture where, for example, the use of neurotoxins in shower gel seems like a completely *rational* idea. Many of the products we view as green may only in fact be green in comparison to the noxious nature of the alternatives. But given the scale of how ecologically, socially, and just overall toxic to our health so many of the products we purchase, ingest, and surround ourselves with on a daily basis truly are, it made me wonder by what metric exactly are we judging those so-called products "green"? And is that a metric that does enough for us and the planet?

Finally, what I didn't want to do in this book was to leave people in a place where they felt helpless. The environmental movement has a nasty habit of overwhelming people with depressing facts that leaves them feeling powerless unless they quit their job, move into a sustainably woven yurt heated only by body heat, and spend their days foraging for food. I was born and raised in New York City, and while my forays into the country have left me reasonably comfortable identifying some plant species, particularly the abundant and tasty ones, if I had to depend on foraging for my survival, I'd be dead inside of a week. Similarly, if the only way I could get involved with the environmental movement was to aspire to some unattainable ideal of being the perfect environmentalist, I wouldn't get involved in the first place. A wise friend once told me that "purity means not getting involved," and I think some people use that bar of perfection to avoid engaging altogether.

In reality, what the environmental movement needs are regular people who work in government, business, and the non-profit realms injecting sustainability in places where it's not currently being discussed. While we do need to be more conscious about what and how much we choose to consume, that consciousness is a starting point, not an ending point. Fortunately, environmentalism is a school with rolling admissions. You can join in at any point and in the ways in which you most feel comfortable.

INTRODUCTION: EMPTO ERGO SUM

People who look through keyholes are apt to get the idea that most things are keyhole shaped.—Unknown

Is the glass half empty, half full, or twice as large as it needs to be?—Unknown

We are at the environmental equivalent of the United States moments from dropping the bomb on Hiroshima. We are Guttenberg before he unveiled his printing press, the ancient residents of Easter Island poised to cut down the last tree, the Bolsheviks just before launching the October Revolution. In short, we are human society on the edge of either environmental collapse or social evolution—and how and what we consume is a critical piece of that picture.

Scientists agree on this much: by nearly every measurable indicator, humanity has wrought enough environmental damage to bring our continued future (in any significant measure) into real question, unless we fundamentally change our relationship with the planet. The issue extends beyond climate change to the concept of global biological diversity. Biological diversity, better known as biodiversity, is the variability of life between and within species and ecosystems, and is increasingly recognized as a crucial indicator of and a beneficial contributor to environmental sustainability. "It is", as the United Nations Environment Programme's Convention on Biological Diversity (CBD) points out, "the combination of life forms and their interactions with each other and with the rest of the environment that has made the Earth a uniquely habitable place for humans. Biodiversity provides a large number of goods and services that sustain our lives."[1]

Biodiversity is the source of our drinking water, the building blocks of our food system, and our primary source of health and recreation. While some argue that in some mythical future there may lay a technological fix allowing us to somehow exist without biodiversity, this is a false argument. Technology is not a replacement for biodiversity because it depends on biodiversity for its source material. Almost a quarter of all prescription drugs, for example, are taken directly from plants or are chemically modified versions of plant substances, with more than half modeled on natural compounds.[2] Every school child learns that aspirin is derived from the Willow tree, but many other medicines share a similar history. For example Taxol, a drug derived from the Pacific Yew tree, has shown promise in the treatment of ovarian and breast cancers.[3] The cholesterol lowering drug Lovostatin is derived from the fungus Aspergillus terreus.[4] The cosmologist Carl Sagan was once quoted as having said, "If you want to make an apple pie from scratch, you must first create the universe." Biodiversity is the universe upon which our technology, though amazing, depends.

And we are destroying it.

In 2010, the Convention on Biological Diversity released *Global Diversity Outlook 3*, a 95-page report detailing the increasing rate at which human behavior is triggering global biodiversity loss and the mass extinctions of not only plants and animals but of entire ecosystems. To give this some context, it's important to note that although species go extinct regularly—neither saber tooth tigers nor dinosaurs currently roam the earth—what's abnormal these days is the rate at which species are going extinct.

Experts estimate that current extinction rates may be up to *1,000* times higher than the normal historical rate. It's not simply that we're killing off many species—we're eradicating a delicate natural balance that took millennia to develop.

The endangered African elephant, for example, beyond being a brilliant animal that communicates ultrasonically and mourns and buries its dead, is also a *keystone* species, which means that it is a species that has a disproportionate effect on its environment in comparison to its size. The African elephant pulls down trees, helping to maintain the savannah landscape it inhabits, breaks up bushes, digs water holes and forge trails. Its droppings, which baboons and birds pick through for undigested seeds and nuts, both helps to spread this natural fertilizer, replenishing depleted soil, as well as serving as a vehicle for seed disposal; some seeds will not germinate unless they have passed through an elephant's digestive system. As the elephant disappears, so too do many of the plants that humans depend on.

In addition, not only are rare and beautiful species and ecosystems such as polar bears and coral reefs disappearing, we are also losing ecosystems that were once so vilified we drained them, as the broad destruction of swamps has only now taught us their value. Rebranded this days as wetlands, these damp boggy environs, preferred by Winnie the Pooh's Eyeore, are natural carbon sinks that store large amounts of the carbon that we spew into the atmosphere, helping to slow down climate change. These diverse ecosystems also play a key role in the water cycle, which in turn provides us with clean drinking water while also providing a natural buffer for our coastlines. Wetlands breakup storms and reduce their effects on land. This is a lesson that the city of New Orleans learned the hard way with Hurricane Katrina. When you combine the rate of biodiversity loss with the destruction of wetlands, the erosion of forests, the increasing rates of desertification, dwindling fresh water supplies, erosion of fish stocks, soil loss, resource depletion, among many other environmental problems, you generate a list so alarming that even the most ardent climate skeptic must begrudgingly admit that we have enough cause to engage in at least *some* worry.

In response to this constant barrage of environmental gloom and doom a meme, or cultural idea, has emerged that the best way of fixing our problems is for each of us to simply consume *differently*. Thus, every day millions of Americans dutifully replace conventional produce with organic, swap Mr. Clean for Seventh Generation, and replace their bottled water with water bottles. Many of us have gotten the message via blogs, television shows, and newspaper and magazine articles that the path to global environmental sustainability is paved by shopping green. This is reflected in the way that we shop—at least 36 percent of us "always" or "regularly" purchase green products according to consumer marketing company Minitel. This percentage has remained steady even during our current recession, despite the fact that green consumer goods often cost more than conventional ones.[5]

All of this provides the comforting message that we can shop ourselves out of our current environmental mess. After all, as an astute college professor I once had pointed out, it's the rare individual who deliberately wants to cause harm. It's the rare farmer who finds joy in raising sick animals, or who revels in poisoning the soil. Similarly, your typical American doesn't want to buy food that sickens the earth, clothes that pollute water supplies, wedding rings that fuel wars, or products that encourage child slavery. When faced with the uncomfortable reality of the detrimental effects of our consumption, most of us do feel guilty. But we continue to consume nonetheless, because behaving differently is often so hard as to be heroic.

Case in point: In much of the United States it's nearly impossible to function without a car. This is a reality that I, a native New Yorker, didn't fully comprehend until I moved to rural Vermont with neither a driver's license nor a car. Suddenly

I was faced with a complete lack of mobility that I had never experienced before. Growing up in New York, I had conquered the mass transit system before I even hit puberty—as a pre-teen I shuttled myself to gymnastics classes, courtesy of two buses, while my parents worked. In Vermont, however, without a car, I was almost completely dependent on my (exceedingly good hearted) roommates to drive me to school, to work, to the supermarket. The few times I cycled the roughly ten hilly miles into town I discovered my lack of physical fitness, and how heavy a five pound bag of potatoes truly is when strapped to one's back, as well as, on another occasion, developing a mild case of hypothermia. Thus, within three months, I had a car and a driver's license, and within nine months, I had a job that required a seventy mile roundtrip daily commute.

Based on my experiences in Vermont, it makes sense, then, that most people would be drawn to the idea of buying better, instead of having to actually embrace a different, and likely more difficult, lifestyle. The threshold for swapping a gas-guzzler for a hybrid is much lower than giving up driving altogether for cycling or walking. Similarly, although it used to be hard to find "green cleaning supplies" or "sustainable water bottles," an increasingly lucrative green industry now makes it simple to locate these items on the shelves of your local supermarket. And this industry is not limited just to water or cleaning supplies. Discovery Communications launched a channel called *Planet Green* featuring shows like "Mean Green Machines" which it describes "as a turbocharged thrill ride jam-packed with the latest, fastest, and greenest vehicles, bikes, and even aircrafts," while Whole Foods has made billions schilling organic chocolate cream filled cookies (aka organic Oreos) and grass fed lamb flown in from New Zealand.

The rise of green industries ties neatly into our attitudes as a nation, as we increasingly define ourselves not by what we do (employment or hobbies), or who we are connected to (friends, families), but by what we buy. Elks lodges, sewing circles, bowling leagues—the sort of formal and informal social connections that used to bind life together—have dwindled. States author Robert Putnam, "Over the course of the last generation or two, a variety of technological, economic and social changes have rendered obsolete the stuff of American social capital."[6] Corporations, media, even our elected officials, no longer refer to the American people as citizens but rather as *consumers*. René Descartes philosophical point *Cogito ergo sum* or *I think, therefore I am*, used to illustrate the idea that somebody wondering whether or not she exists is itself proof that she in fact does exist has been replaced with *Empto ergo sum* or *I shop, therefore I am*. In a country where many of us pray to different gods, and some of us don't pray at all, where some of us are urban and others are rural, where some vote and others don't, and, with an ever increasing number of media outlets catering to our precise worldview, meaning we rarely watch the same shows, our collective consumption is the one thing that binds us together.

Taking a deeper look at that consumption—especially the kind of consumption we believe will save us from ecological disaster—is not just an intellectual exercise. It's about hope. It's about clarity. It is the sunlight that former Supreme Court justice Louis Brandeis once called the best disinfectant. We need to know how green these so-called green alternatives really are? How much can shopping differently really achieve when it comes to saving our planet? Can we shop ourselves green? Or is it, as Einstein once stated, impossible to solve our problems with the same thinking (and behaviors) that we used when we created them? Does what we buy matter more than how much we buy? And if, as the evidence strongly suggests, the volume of our consumption is what matters, can we as a society, with an economic system and a culture dependent on constantly consuming more, ever be content with buying less?

PART I—HOW GREEN IS GREEN?

The things we throw out most readily—without thought or hesitation—will be the very things that will prove to be the most lasting substance known to any civilization of human being. How is it that we came to dispose so readily of something so permanent, when so many generations that preceded us worked so mightily to preserve even those things that are fleeting?—Patrick J. Deneen

1. GREEN IS THE NEW BLACK

> *As a fashion designer, I was always aware that I was not an artist, because I was creating something that was made to be sold, marketed, used, and ultimately discarded.*—Tom Ford

> *I don't design clothes, I design dreams.*—Ralph Lauren

> *Fashion is what you adopt when you don't know who you are.* —Quentin Crisp

Why is Loomstate, a brand of jeans completely at home nestled among the nine-stories of polished wood, mosaic marble, and gold leaf trimming laid upon the sweeping ceilings that comprise the 230,000 square foot Madison Avenue flagship location of Barneys, so special? ceilings that comprise the 230,000 square foot Madison Avenue flagship location of Barneys, so special? Loomstate's jeans, a trendy mix of hip huggers, slim fit jeans with dark washes, and wide-legged boyfriend jeans, are not markedly different than the other jeans with which they share a floor at the store. Nor is their price tag remarkable. Although Loomstate jeans routinely sell for upwards of $100 per pair, most committed fashionistas wouldn't bat an eyelash at plunking down even twice that amount for the right pair of designer dungarees.

Loomstate's pedigree is what makes it so unique, as the company's full name—Loomstate Organics—marks it as part of an increasing crop of businesses specializing in 100% organic cotton, naturally dyed 'sustainable' fashion. The goal of companies like

Loomstate is to reposition green fashion away from its typical consumer—one who was typically at home on small back-to-the-land styled farms, at chill music festivals, or at the still rare vegan restaurant—to a customer who is far more comfortable stalking the streets of Manhattan or walking the runways of Milan.

Stereotypically, sustainable clothing—rough, itchy hemp fabrics, coarsely dyed, if dyed at all, in earth hues of burnt umber, weak ochre and tepid sienna—has been the province of visible hippies; it's the sort of clothes familiar to anyone who has ever seen footage of the original Woodstock Festival. It has also only ever comprised a small percentage of the overall clothing market and was not a viable avenue of pursuit for anyone serious about fashion. This new wave of sustainable fashion, by contrast, featuring rugged fleece made from recycled soda bottles, silky slacks made from spun bamboo, and yes the aforementioned organic cotton jeans, is an outgrowth of our increasing awareness of the relationship between our consumption and the destruction it's causing the planet. This awareness, perhaps most visible in food, has increasingly trickled into other segments of the consumer market, including clothing. As an example, Jonathan Meztler, founder of the clothing brand Anti-Eco, which sells organic, fair-trade t-shirts with sarcastic slogans such as "Be Organic Eat an Organ" over a picture of a human heart, and "100% genetically modified organism" beneath a picture of a fish with human feet, admits that he was inspired to create his line after watching the 2008 documentary *Food Inc.,* which took a scathing look at the havoc corporate farming plays on the environment, animals, and people.

There is now a sustainable niche for every one of your clothing needs and desires. You can buy sustainable socks made from wool reclaimed from old sweaters; odor resistant t-shirts spun from bamboo; new wedding dresses made from material salvaged from old wedding dresses; and for those with especially deep pockets, high end brands such as Theory and Stella McCartney have launched "conscious" lines.[1] Similarly, headlines such as "Green is the New Black" and "Absolutely ethical, darling!" are popping up on the pages of fashion magazines, illustrating a fundamental shift in the sustainable clothing market.[2] There have been sustainable and/or ethical fashion shows on the runways of Paris, London and New York, while distinctly middle of the road retailers such as the Gap and H&M have taken to selling t-shirts made from sustainable materials.

A belle weather year in this regard was 2007, which was the first year that the sustainable fashion market was cohesive enough to estimate global retail sales—some $3 billion. Although it's a significant sum of money, it still only made up 1 percent of the total fashion market.[3] Overall, only 18 percent of consumers are even aware that eco-fashion exists. These numbers, taken together, suggest that sustainable fashion is less a movement geared towards ushering in true sustainability and more a niche market that allows a segment of consumers to assuage their eco-guilt. Case in point: In April 2007, conventional accessories designer Anya Hindmarch unveiled a beige cotton bag emblazoned with the saying "I Am Not A Plastic Bag." The idea was to bring attention to the sheer volume of plastic bags that were used briefly to lug home groceries or other such purchases, and then rapidly discarded. In the United States, the average person uses between 350 and 500 plastic bags each year, totaling some 1 billion bags per annum. These bags never biodegrade, and ultimately end up clogging rivers, streams, oceans and the digestive tracts of marine life, most notably sea turtles, which mistake the bags for jellyfish. Yet despite the fact that these "awareness-raising" bags sold out everywhere and were later found on ebay for five to ten times their original store price of $15, the national use of plastic bags has not declined appreciably over the past five years. Ironically, the bags themselves have disappeared, as they're no longer considered en vogue.

This idea, that eco-fashion is less about environmental sustainability and more about mitigating guilt, becomes more compelling when one looks at the darling of the sustainable fashion world, organic cotton. Comprising roughly 68 percent of the sustainable fabric market, organic cotton is so significant that the Wildlife Conservation Society (WCS), of Bronx Zoo fame, and the sustainable brand Edun, begun by U2 front man Bono along with his wife Ali Lewson, collaborated to give cotton its own initiative—the Conservation Cotton Initiative. The Initiative operates with the stated goal of improving the livelihoods of communities in Africa by investing in sustainably harvested, particularly organic "conservation cotton."

Unlike other so-called "earth friendly" fabrics such as bamboo or polyester spun from soda bottles, organic cotton is functionally identical to conventional cotton. Thus, there is no learning curve involved in modifying or using the material—the full brunt of the costs, risks, and expertise of the material lies solely in the domain of the farmers who grow it. In other words, to a designer, organic cotton is conventional cotton with a veneer of sustainability. And in many ways—particularly when it comes to pesticide use—organic cotton is better than conventional. Although cotton crops occupy just 3 percent of global cropland, they consume 25 percent of the world's pesticides and fertilizers, posing a serious threat to the health of farmers and to the larger environment.[4] The heavy use of artificial fertilizers often pollutes rivers and streams, in the process killing off fish that people depend upon for food. Many cotton farmers, located in developing nations, use pesticides that have been either banned or strictly curtailed in developed nations, such as *endosulfan*, which poisons the nervous system and causes cancer. Quite often, these chemicals seep into the ground water, where they are then drunk with breakfast, rinse the vegetables that make up lunch, and are boiled into the evening stew. Children, whose nervous systems are still developing, can suffer a lifetime of ill effects from this constant low level exposure, while the farmers who experience direct exposure through application can suffer even more dramatic health consequences. Even the end consumer suffers as pesticides linger in the fabric, and miniscule amounts are absorbed through the skin.

While organic cotton is certainly superior to its conventional counterparts because it uses a lower amount of pesticides, the reality is that cotton's widespread global cultivation cannot be called anything near sustainable, even if we could completely remove pesticides from the mix. Primarily grown in dry tropical and subtropical climates, cotton needs warm temperatures and lots of water to flourish. This is a problem, because the places where cotton is grown—China, India, Pakistan, the Southern United States and Uzbekistan—are places that are short on water. To understand why cotton's insatiable thirst is problematic, it helps to understand the concept of virtual water. Also known as "embedded water" or "embodied water" the idea was created by Jonathan Anthony Allan of Kings College London as a way of measuring how much water is embedded in the production and trade of consumer products. For example, it takes approximately 10 gallons of water to make one slice of bread. For a single cotton t-shirt? A whopping 400 gallons of water. This wouldn't be much of a problem if the water for cotton came from rainfall (commonly known as green water). If this were the case, most of the water used to grow cotton would remain within the local ecosystem, allowing the water cycle to continue.

However, although the earth is more than 71 percent water, most of that—a startling 97 percent—is salt water. The rest of us depend on the meager 3 percent of water that is fresh water. The reason we are able to subsist on such a small percentage of the world's water is because of the water cycle—a term that describes the continuous movement of water on, above, and below the surface of the earth in what is the ultimate act of recycling. The water that we drink today was drunk by our grandparents and will be drunk by our grandchildren.

In some places, however—such as in large swathes of Pakistan, especially where cotton is grown—rainfall is relatively scarce. Instead of turning to the sky for water, people in these places depend on ground water supplies that are slowly fed from a series of hidden rivers and streams. Sometimes, such as in parts of China, people depend on ground water that used to be fed by rivers and streams which have long since dried up. These water supplies, trapped underground, have remained, but once consumed, they will not be renewed. In both these cases, this water, called blue water, if not carefully used, is finite: once it's gone, it's gone

Figure 1

forever. This incredibly scarce resource is what is used to water 53 percent of the world's cotton fields, producing some 73 percent of global cotton production.[5]

To understand what cotton production can do to an ecosystem, one only has to go as far as Eastern Europe to visit the Aral Sea. Nestled between Kazakhstan to the north and Uzbekistan to the south, the Aral Sea used to be one of the four largest lakes in the world, registering in at a whopping 26,300 square miles—roughly 52 times the size of the city of Los Angeles. At one time, The Aral Sea "was home to 24 native species of fish. Its waters encompassed over 1100 islands forming countless lagoons and shallow straits, and on the open seas, fleets of trawlers landed 40,000 tons of fish every year."[6] During the 1960's, however, the then USSR began diverting two key rivers—the Amu Darya and the Syr Darya—which fed into the Aral, in a bid to make Uzbekistan the center of Soviet cotton production. A half century later, the Aral is 10 percent of its former size, its water is 600 percent saltier, and its fishing industry is no more. The massive trawlers, which once hauled some 40,000 tons of fish every year, lay rusting in plain air, dotting the roughly 15,500 thousand square miles (akin to some 6 million football fields) of now exposed sea bed.[7] The Aral Sea is all but dead—and cotton killed it.

Apart from wreaking havoc on local ecosystems, reducing drinking water supplies in places where water is already scarce (according to the World Water Council, some 1.1 billion people lack access to safe drinking supplies, with 3,900 children dying daily from water borne diseases), cotton has another unsustainable flaw. Points out Stephen Veryser of the Tanzanian based eco-agriculture organization Evergreen Agriculture Tanzania (or simply EAT!):

> You can't eat cotton. Since cotton isn't processed locally the market is subject to the volatile international pricing swings. In typical fashion, if supply is short worldwide, prices jump for a year, then lots of farmers are enticed to switch over to cotton and supply booms the next year, thus crashing prices. The problem with this, aside from bankrupting the farmers, is that they really can't do anything with that couple of tons of soft fluffy stuff (at least rice, for example, they could save, eat, sell bit by bit to get by while waiting for prices to rise).

This isn't an issue limited to developing nations. A March 2011 *New York Times* article explained that because of increasing demand, farmers from North Carolina to Texas, due to an uptick in cotton prices, are swapping corn and wheat for cotton even as global food prices soar. “It’s good for the farmer,” the article states, “but from a humanitarian perspective it’s kind of scary... Those people in poor countries that have a hard time affording food, they’re going to be even less able to afford it now.”[8]

Ultimately, the negative ecological and social effects of cotton aren’t the fashion industries’ biggest problem when it comes to achieving sustainability. Simply put, fashion—green or otherwise—is unsustainable because it is an industry that depends on people constantly buying more of what it has to offer, regardless of actual need. Once upon a time, people actually repaired their clothing—they stitched seams, darned hemlines, and patched elbows. Back then, clothes were expensive and fabricated to last. Consequently, as recently as sixty years ago, people owned far fewer clothes than your modern American’s bursting at the seams wardrobe. Clothes today are meant to be worn briefly, a hiccup in time between the arduous task of being wrested into form from a dizzying array of raw materials—seed, soil, water, oil—and being carelessly returned to the earth as waste. The fashion industry depends on this constant, incessant change to feed its bottom line. Thus, the garments pressed into consumer hands by fashion retailers such as H&M and Zara are purposefully designed not for longevity, but for rapid obsolescence. They are meant to be worn no more than ten times and then be tossed out.[9] As a result, since 1994, municipal textile waste has grown 87 percent as each year, Americans throw out more than 12.37 million tons of material. In that same time span, our population only grew by 14 percent. In other words, we’re all consuming more clothes.

One of the main reasons we’re consuming so much clothing is because while fashion likes to position itself as art, it is a consumer art, bound as much by the constant drumbeat of the business cycle as much, or perhaps more so, than by aesthetics. Designers have five seasons worth of fashion to sell—Fall, Holiday, Resort, Spring, and Summer—and they do it by convincing us that we are what we wear and then actively and perpetually changing what that aesthetic means.[10] This season long hemlines are popular; next season, designers will reintroduce the mini. This pattern of continual change makes the fact that we purchased this pair of slacks, or those pair of shoes, two seasons ago, clearly evident. Clothes are a means of protection from the elements, but fashion is an attempt to carve a visible identity for ourselves, to define ourselves from the outside in and to shape how others look and perceive us.[11] This is why so many of us find it hard to wear "last year's fashions" despite the fact that they have changed in neither form nor function. "This dissatisfaction," writes the fashion social critic Zygmunt Bauman, "doesn't come necessarily

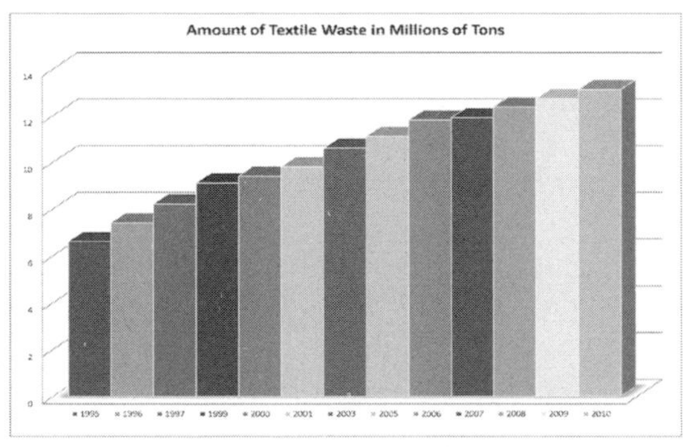

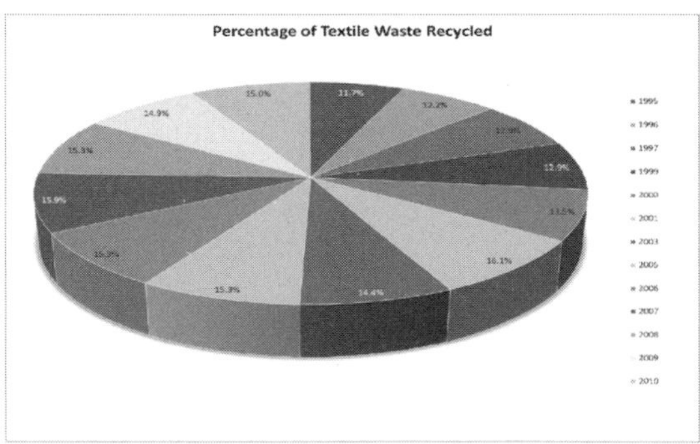

from the clothes themselves, but rather, what the clothes represent." And since we're not the ones doing the defining—the designers are—it becomes much easier to discard and purchase with the rapidly changing tides of fashion.

However, things may finally be changing. With a disdain for fashion and a strong do it yourself ethic, Wendy Tremayne is on the fringe edge of an idea that is gaining increasing traction—namely that the most sustainable thing we can do within the fashion industry is to stop buying, or at least to buy less. Wendy founded Swap-O-Rama-Rama, a series of clothing swaps and do-it yourself-workshops, as a way of pushing back against the idea of an industry dictated aesthetic and of shopping as political action. The swap-o-rama website states that, "When you attend the swap bring at least one bag of your unwanted clothing. Every swap begins with a giant collective pile of clothing, the unwanted clothing of all who attend. Everyone is welcome to dive in and find their next new/used items from the pile. Take as little or as much clothing from this pile as you like, it's all free."[12] Participants then go to a variety of do-it-yourself stations which empowers them to rip, dye, stencil, and otherwise personalize their new-to-them items. Wendy argues that "One of the biggest problems with fashion is that we are pushed to purchase objects that at the end of the day have little meaning. Stuff that has little meaning becomes easy to dispose of—it quickly becomes waste. When you imbue a product with meaning, for example by making it yourself, you fabricate a maker lifestyle that doesn't produce waste."

In October 2011, Patagonia, an outdoor and lifestyle clothing retailer with a strong emphasis on sustainability—it was Patagonia who helped to normalize both organic cotton and fleece made from recycled soda bottles—unveiled their Common Threads Initiative, which, to paraphrase their own website [emphasis added]

> **reduce the quantity of clothing items their consumers will need to buy** by using quality materials solidly constructed. Repair garment failures such as failed zippers in garments that otherwise have a lot of life in them. Reuse items by facilitating a way for consumers to sell, trade, or donate an item they no longer have need for, and then finally, if all else fails, recycle.

When a major retailer with annual sales of more than quarter of a billion dollar says that one of the most sustainable things that we as consumers can do is to buy less, perhaps we should listen.

2.HOW WE EAT

> *The most fundamental requirement for survival is food. Hence, how and where food is grown is foundational to an economics for community.*—Herman Daly and John Cobb

> *We are living in a world today where lemonade is made from artificial flavors and furniture polish is made from real lemons.* —Alfred E. Newman

> *When I add a spoon of honey to my tea, I give thanks to a dozen bees for the work of their whole lives. When my finger sweeps the final drop of sweetness from the jar, I know we've enjoyed the nectar from over a million flowers. This is what honey is: the souls of flowers, a food to please the gods. Honeyeaters know that to have a joyful heart one must live life like the bees, sipping the sweet nectar from each moment as it blooms. And Life, like the world of honey, has its enchantments and stings...*—Ingrid Goff-Maidoff

For many Americans, the Mississippi River's 2,320 rambling miles—beginning in Wisconsin and weaving its way through Illinois, Missouri, Arkansas, and, of course, Mississippi, before heading to its final resting place in Louisiana where it releases its turbid waters into the Gulf of Mexico—is synonymous with one man, Mark Twain. Born Samuel Clemens, Twain was from birth until death a Mississippi River man, going so far as to rename himself after a Mississippi River term meaning "mark number two" or the second mark on the line that measures depth signifying two fathoms, or twelve feet. Twelve feet signified a safe passing depth for the steamboat he would drive for four years, before his piloting career was cut short by the Civil War.

Under Twain's steady pen, tales such as *The Adventures of Huckleberry Finn*, *The Tragedy of Pudd'nhead Wilson*, and of course, *Life on the Mississippi*, allowed countless readers to get to know the beauty of the Mississippi. The man who once famously told *The Atlantic Monthly*, "When I was a boy, there was but one permanent ambition among my comrades in our village on the west bank of the Mississippi River. That was, to be a steamboatman," brought the Mississippi River alive to generations of Americans. It's a shame that the current generation of Americans is killing it.

Each year in the Upper Mississippi River Basin, the 121.5 million acres between north central Minnesota and the confluence of the Mississippi and Ohio rivers, some 47 million acres of cropland are fertilized and treated with weed controlling herbicides, while another 20 million acres are treated with pesticides.[1] The chemicals don't just stay on the field, however; they sink into the soil where they join underground tributaries, or get washed into waterways with the rain. Eventually they feed into the Mississippi, heading further and further south and growing ever more concentrated, until they unleash the full fury of man's agricultural assault into the Gulf of Mexico.

As a result, for the animals in the Gulf, summer, a season most of us associate with life, brings death as the nitrogen from the fertilizer that we use on our crops spurs the rapid growth of algae. Having a short life span, the algae quickly dies, leaving behind a high concentration of material that sucks the oxygen out of the water as it decays, sending those creatures that can escape scurrying for safety and leaving those who are too slow or too stationary behind to die. First mapped in 1985, each summer this "dead zone" grows slightly larger—today it is roughly the size of the state of New Hampshire—before shrinking again when autumn brings waves and winds to oxygenate the water.

The panoply of toxic chemicals and fertilizers that inhabit the Gulf of Mexico and the similarly blighted Chesapeake Bay in Maryland are byproducts of industrial agriculture, a techno-scientific-based system that uses economic and political structures to shift agriculture from its inherent ecological base to one that relies heavily on the use of artificial pesticides, herbicides, fungicides, fertilizers and genetically modified organisms (GMOs). It is a system in which the banal—a farmer near China's Danyang City planting watermelon—can turn into the bizarre new normal as those watermelons explode in size after the overuse and misapplication of a "growth accelerator."[2] In this case, the growth accelerator, forchlorfenuron, has also been shown to interfere with the division of human cells in ways that have been linked to cancer and neurological diseases.[3]

In much the same way that the industrial revolution turned so many people into de facto factory workers, industrial agriculture attempts to turn the biological process of growing food into mechanized factory work, arguing that in doing so we can grow more food, faster, and thus better feed the planet's human population. We are told that industrial agriculture is the best way, is in fact the only way, we will ever mitigate global hunger. And yet, at the same time, it is a food system that often times seems more efficient at harming the environment than it does at feeding people. For example, the animals that are part of the system are mainly housed in Concentrated Animal Feeding Operations (CAFOs), in which poultry, pigs, cattle or other animals are penned into containers so small that many have to be pumped with a regular low-dose of antibiotics to ward off illnesses. In addition to being cruel to the animals, CAFOs are also unfit for anyone who has the misfortune of living in the vicinity of such a facility. In such operations, livestock waste is not cured into manure where it can be plowed back into the land as fertilizer, but rather stored in giant lagoons where it becomes a health hazard. In 2009, a hog farmer in Hayfield, Minnesota was thrown some forty feet in an explosion caused by methane gas from a manure pit on his farm.[4] Less sensational, but far more harmful, these pits can leach viruses, nitrogen, and heavy metals into nearby ground water and create air so toxic that it causes respiratory distress.

Industrial agriculture also consumes tremendous amounts of water. According to the US Department of Agriculture, agriculture is the main user of ground and surface water in this country, accounting for 80 percent of the nation's water consumption, and over 90 percent in many western states.[5] To access all this ground water, irrigation systems are removing water from reservoirs and ground water systems far faster than they can be replenished. This is seen most strikingly in the case of the Ogallala Aquifer. Named after the Ogala Sioux tribe—meaning to "scatter one's own"—the Ogallala is the world's largest underground reservoir, spanning some 174,000 square miles. Reaching as far north as South Dakota, as far south as Texas and as far west as Wyoming, it forms a water supply so vast it could fill Lake Erie nine times over. If spread across the United States, the Ogallala would flood all fifty states with roughly a foot and a half of water.[6] Nationwide, it supplies water for 19 percent of our nation's cotton and 15 percent of our corn, as well as providing 70 percent of the water supply for the state of Kansas.

And yet, this seemingly endless body of water is rapidly disappearing. In some places it is already gone. The Texas panhandle town of Happy, though never a bustling metropolis, was once, well, happy, due in large part to a cattle ranching lifestyle made possible by wells dug into the Ogallala in the 1950s. Those wells, however, have since dried up. Instead of wheat waving beneath the Texas sky and cows mewling in the distance, what remains of the town are dried up crops and lots and lots of dust, reminiscent of the Dust Bowl that ravaged the American and Canadian plains in the 1930s. And, as in the Dust Bowl era, in which people who could no longer eke out a subsistence living fled for greener pastures, people are leaving Happy, as with each passing year, the town's population declines by ten percent.[7] Unfortunately, Happy is increasingly finding itself in grim company. Already in towns such as the ironically named Garden City, a farm community in Southern Kansas roughly 180 miles west of Wichita, the Ogallala is in rapid retreat, forcing farmers to tackle the increasingly impossible task of working their land while depending on less and less water.[8] This is a tragedy that will be replicated in towns across Oklahoma, Kansas and in already water strapped Colorado. Says David Bauer, program manager for the Ogallala Initiative, a project funded by the United States Department of Agriculture-Agricultural Research Service (USDA-ARS) to study the aquifer, "The Ogallala supply is going to run out and the Plains will become uneconomical to farm…That is beyond reasonable argument. Our goal now is to engineer a soft landing. That's all we can do."[9] And, argues Bauer, the transformation is going to happen quickly, "You go to areas where the aquifer has been depleted, [they] look pretty poor now, and it only takes a few years."[10]

The reason for this problem is that groundwater, unlike surface water which is dynamic and rapidly renewing, is slow to replenish, as it is often formed by ancient waters from glaciers held underground for thousands, in some cases millions, of years. Once depleted, it will take almost as much time to refill. The Ogallala Aquifer, for example, if depleted, would take six thousand years to replenish itself.[11] Yet, in just the past half century, "we have drawn the Ogallala level down from an average of 240 ft to about 80."[12] Ninety percent of the water removed from the Ogallala—some five trillion gallons—is removed for agriculture.[13] According to Food and Water Watch, over the past fifty years, the aquifer has lost 65 trillion gallons of water in storage, enough to supply all of the homes and businesses in Washington, D.C. with drinking water for more than 1000 years.[14] Similarly, the Colorado River, whose steady pace was the invisible hand that carved the Grand

Canyon some 17 million years ago, has been reduced by agriculture from a thundering, rushing river to one that dribbles into its final destination, Mexico's Gulf of California, located on the Baja Peninsula. According to the nonprofit organization, Save the Colorado River, a startling 78 percent of the river's flow, almost 4 trillion gallons, is diverted for agriculture.[15] The Colorado River's waters are redirected via the seemingly, ironically named All-American Canal to grow fruits and vegetables, including water thirsty crops such as melons, in the deserts of Southern California's Imperial Valley. It is a conceit of industrial agriculture to think that we could transform some half a million acres of desert into lush farmland without upsetting an ecological balance that had existed for millennia.

In addition to depleting and polluting water supplies, industrial agriculture eradicates global biodiversity, depletes and erodes soil and, points out the Union of Concern Scientists, the large, highly specialized, mechanistic methods by which we run factory farms in the United States require large inputs of fossil fuels, pesticides, herbicides, and insecticides, as well as synthetic fertilizers derived from oil. Simply put, this system is unsustainable. A 2002 study by the John Hopkins Bloomberg School of Public Health showed that for each calorie of edible food our current system requires three calories of energy, and that number excludes the energy used in processing and transporting the food.[16] Overall, agriculture consumes 17 percent of the total amount of fossil fuels used in the United States.[17]

And yet, even as our scientific knowledge of what conventional chemical and genetically modified agriculture is increasingly doing to humans, the land, and biodiversity, this hasn't stopped our collective culture from continuing to hitch our survival wagons to the horses of chemical and GMO agriculture. For example, the Bill and Melinda Gates Foundation is contributing millions of dollars in support of genetically modified technologies such as drought tolerant maize to help usher in an agricultural revolution in sub-Saharan Africa buoyed by the belief that the future for sustainable development lies in genetically modified technologies.[18] Never mind the fact that the last "successful" agricultural revolution in a developing nation—the Green Revolution in India—left that country with tainted ground water supplies, depleted soil, plenty of hungry people, and was the driving force behind the population exodus from rural areas to the urban slums.[19]

The United States, though heavily invested in GMO technology for well over a decade—as of 2011, 94 percent of soybeans and 88 percent of corn planted in this country were genetically modified—has not been able to show that this method of growing crops has resulted in a reduced use of pesticides, insecticides, or water usage.[20] Quite the opposite, as some studies have shown that genetically modified plants designed to be resistant to herbicides (thus allowing farmers to spray less) have in fact fueled an upswing in the use of other pesticides. Take for example the widespread use of glyphosate tolerant crops. Glyphosate, better known by its commercial name of "Round Up" is an herbicide that's especially effective at killing the broad leaf weeds and grasses that target corn and soy fields. Under normal situations, if you sprayed a corn field with glyphosate, the corn would die alongside the weeds. However, the biotech company Monsanto has genetically modified certain crops, including soy beans and corn, to be resistant to glyphosate, enabling farmers to spray their entire field while selectively killing only the weeds. While this sounds like a solution, in fact it is not, as the weeds have rapidly evolved to resist glyphosate.

Although this reality has only recently begun to receive widespread recognition, such as in a 2010 *New York Times* article entitled "Rise of the Superweeds" others have been sounding the alarm for much longer.[21] Bob Hartzler, a weed scientist at Iowa State University, was warning about the rise of Round up-resistant weeds as early as January of 2003.[22] Similarly, reports were emerging the following year that the American-financed fumigation of Colombia's coca fields with glyphosate, as part of US war on drugs (and specifically on Colombia's position as a leading supplier of cocaine) had created its own Frankenstein—a strain of coca alternatively known as supercoca or la millonaria that not only had more leaves than your normal coca plant but was also glyphosate resistant.[23] In other words, the American government had accidentally created a variety of coca that was not only more abundant, but also harder to kill.

Back at home, farmers today are increasingly finding that when they spray their fields with glyphosate, weeds still remain, forcing them to then use other herbicides.[24] Rather than reducing pesticide use, GMO's seem to be hastening it. According to the 2010 Times article, "Just as the heavy use of antibiotics contributed to the rise of drug-resistant supergerms, American farmers' near-ubiquitous use of the weedkiller Roundup has led to the rapid growth of tenacious new superweeds." This statement is borne out by a 2009 report published by the Colorado based nonprofit organization, The Organic Center, which claims that from 1996 to 2008, the use of GMO plants led to an increased herbicide use of 383 million pounds over what would have been used had GMO technology never been used in the first place.[25] As Matt LIebman, the H.A. Wallace Chair for Sustainable Agriculture at Iowa State University in Ames states, the heavy reliance and rotation between glyphosate resistant corn and glypohosate resistant soy have created "good conditions for rapid selection of herbicide resistance." In the meantime, farmers are being forced to spray their fields with increasingly toxic herbicides, as well as returning to more labor and water-intensive methods such as regular plowing.[26]

Given that, for most people, the understanding that the heavy use of artificial pesticides and fertilizers might be problematic still remains a novel idea, it can be hard to believe that this experimentation with creating a manmade sustainable food system has been going on for over a century. Over 100 years ago, in 1909, German chemist Fritz Haber developed the technique to produce ammonia from atmospheric nitrogen. This process was then purchased by the German chemical company BASF, and chemist and engineer Carl Bosch was given the demanding task of transforming Haber's technique from a tabletop reaction to one that could be reproduced on a mass scale. His success and the resulting technique, which allowed for the development of cheap, easy to transport artificial fertilizers, was named the Haber-Bosch process, and would earn both Haber (in 1918) and Bosch (in 1931) the Nobel Prize in Chemistry, as well as usher in the modern agricultural era.

Around the same time that Bosch was refitting Haber's techniques for practical use, chemists were hard at work developing chlorine gasses to be used as weapons during World War I. By World War II, scientists had gone even further, modifying the rudimentary, though effective, gasses of the first world war, which had often been little more than particles suspended in air, to create a far more deadlier class of chloride gases such as cyanogen chloride, a corrosive, colorless gas with a biting odor that blocks the ability of red blood cells to transport oxygen within the body, dooming those exposed to a choking death by asphyxiation. With the end of World War II, the chemical companies were in need of new ways of expanding their market, and turned to agriculture, developing their chlorine-based gasses into the first wave of artificial pesticides, including the infamous DDT.

Almost immediately, however, a countermovement was formed—the organic food movement. The International Federation of Organic Agriculture Movements defines organic agriculture as a

> production system that sustains the health of soils, ecosystems and people. It relies on ecological processes, biodiversity and cycles adapted to local conditions, rather

> than the use of inputs with adverse effects. Organic agriculture combines tradition, innovation and science to benefit the shared environment and promote fair relationships and a good quality of life for all involved.[27]

Although agriculture without artificial pesticides and fertilizers was the norm for millennia before the industrial agricultural age, English botanist Sir Albert Howard is generally regarded as the father of modern organic agriculture, for codifying agriculture into a specific set of principles and behaviors. Howard was heavily inspired by his experiences as the Imperial Economic Botanist to the Government of India from 1905 to 1924, setting down the lessons he learned in two books, 1940's *An Agricultural Testament*, and in 1945's *Farming and Gardening for Health or Disease* which was republished in 1947 as *The Soil and Health: A Study of Organic Agriculture.*

From a practical perspective, today organic agriculture is defined as a system that strictly limits the use of synthetic pesticides, chemical fertilizers, antibiotics, food additives, processing aids and other inputs, and completely prohibits the use of genetically modified organisms and the irradiation of products. Organic farming includes numerous subsets such as biodynamic farming, which was inspired by a series of lectures on agriculture given by philosopher Rudolf Steiner in 1924. Biodynamic doesn't simply eschew the use of artificial pesticides, fertilizers and pesticides, but also encourages farmers to treat the entire farm as a single unified organism and in doing so emphasizes the integration of crops and lifecycle, maintenance of soil, and nutrient cycling. Similarly, agro-ecology, which encompasses techniques such as permaculture and agroforestry (an integrated approach to that combines agricultural and forestry techniques—such as coffee grown in the shade of other trees—to produce food in healthy, sustainable and productive ways), though not strictly organic, borrows heavily from the organic application of ecological science to enhance crop yield.

Proponents of organic farming and its subsets have argued for decades that food grown with synthetic fertilizers and pesticides is less wholesome, negatively affects the environment and is less resilient to ecological hiccups such as droughts, heat waves, and floods. For nearly as long, proponents of industrial agriculture have argued that the environmental problems associated with artificial fertilizers and pesticides can be mitigated, that there is no evidence that organic food is more nutritious, that genetic technologies could easily deal with climatic events, and that while organic may be good for some people—most notably those who can afford to purchase it—to feed a growing world population, we need the more robust technologies associated with industrial agriculture.

Increasingly, the evidence suggests that the organic proponents were right. For example, a 2009 review in the journal *Agronomy for Sustainable Development*, analyzing the major data studies assessing the nutritional component of organic foods, found that on balance, organic plant products have more minerals and anti-oxidant micronutrients such as phenolys, as well as more polyunsaturated fats than their conventional counterparts.[28] Similarly, a June 2002 report in the journal Food Additives and Contaminants analyzed test data on pesticide residues in organic and non-organic foods from three separate sources—Consumers Union, the USDA, and the California Department of Pesticide Regulation—and found that organic foods contain lower levels of pesticides than their conventional cousins. [29] Further, a 2006 study published in the journal *Environmental Health Perspectives* found that organic diets significantly lowered children's exposure to organophosphorus pesticides, a group of pesticides known to cause negative neurological effects.[30] A 2010 study out of the University of Washington comparing strawberries grown on conventional fields with those grown on organic fields (with the organic fields abutting the conventional fields to limit the microclimatic effects) found that the organic strawberries not only contained higher levels of vitamin C and antioxidants, but that the organic strawberry plants were healthier and less likely to be plagued by post-harvest fungal rots.[31] The organic strawberries also left the soil healthier, as the anti-fungal agents and pesticides conventional farmers routinely spray their fields with deplete the soil of nutrients. And perhaps most curiously, DNA analysis showed that the organic soil had significantly higher genetic diversity—the very thing we need to help protect us against changing environmental situations. In other words, organic farming manages to produce healthy, nourishing food without the use of ecologically toxic chemicals, in the process reducing the quantity of fossil fuels that is used.

At the same time, an increasing body of research has linked the herbicides and pesticides used in conventional foods to significant negative health outcomes. While epidemiology is an incredibly nuanced and difficult field of science in which to prove causal relationships (which is why tobacco companies were able to argue for so long that their cigarettes did not cause cancer), the amount of correlative evidence suggesting that something is amiss with industrial agriculture is staggering. For example, while farmers in general have lower rates of "lifestyle" cancers—that is lung, esophagus, bladder, and colon cancers—due likely to better diet, increased exercise, and a lower rate of smoking, they have higher rates of leukemia, non-Hodgkin lymphoma, multiple myeloma, and soft tissue sarcoma, as well as cancers of the stomach, brain, and prostate.[32] According to the National Institutes of Health,

> Farmers, farm workers, and farm family members may be exposed to substances such as pesticides, engine exhausts, solvents, dusts, animal viruses, fertilizers, fuels, and specific microbes that may account for these elevated cancer rates. However, human studies reported to date have not allowed researchers to sort out which of these factors may be linked to which cancer types.[33]

In addition, children are also the unwitting victims of conventional agriculture, particularly in regards to one of the major problems they face today, obesity. A study by Spanish scientists found that the more pesticides children were exposed to as fetuses, the more likely they were to be overweight, while a 2008 study out of Belgium found that children exposed to higher levels of PCBs and DDE (a breakdown product of the pesticide DDT) before birth were fatter than those exposed to lower levels.[34,35] A study conducted by the Mayo Clinic showed that when pregnant rats were exposed to the organophosphorothionate pesticide chlorpyrifos, one of the most commonly used pesticides, their offspring ended up on average 10.5 percent heavier and 12 percent larger than their control (non-exposed) cousins.[36]

The most damning nail in the industrial agriculture coffin, however, is that it fails in its most basic claim, namely in its ability to feed large amounts of people. According to the Food and Agriculture Organization of the United Nations, 925 million people, representing some 15 percent of the global population, are undernourished. Worldwide, there are more hungry people today than the combined populations of the United States, Canada, and the twenty-seven countries that comprise the European Union.[37] Chronic hunger weakens the immune system, making these individuals more susceptible to disease. Undernourished children grow more slowly, both physically and mentally, while mothers who are chronically hungry give birth to weak, underweight babies while simultaneously increasing their own risk for death in childbirth. Given that food underpins health, it is therefore unsurprising that worldwide hunger and related diseases claims more lives than AIDS, malaria and tuberculosis combined.[38] It is a truism that inspires the Haitian proverb, "giving people medicine and not giving them food is like washing your hands and drying them in the dirt."

In 2011, Olivier De Schutter, UN Special Rapporteur on the

Right to Food, issued a report stating that the future of sustainable development lie not in chemical agriculture, but rather in sustainable agricultural techniques.[39] According to De Schutter,

> Today's scientific evidence demonstrates that agro-ecological methods outperform the use of chemical fertilizers in boosting food production where the hungry live—especially in unfavorable environments. To date, agro-ecological projects have shown an average crop yield increase of 80% in 57 developing countries, with an average increase of 116% for all African projects. Recent projects conducted in 20 African countries demonstrated a doubling of crop yields over a period of 3-10 years.[40]

Sustainable agriculture does all of this while maintaining climatic resilience and without polluting ground water supplies. By contrast, GMO technologies have yet to be proven to increase yields in practice.[41] As the report concludes, "Conventional farming relies on expensive inputs, fuels climate change and is not resilient to climatic shocks. It simply is not the best choice anymore." In other words, in many of the ways that matter, organic agriculture is green.

And yet even as De Schutter lays out what seems to be definitive proof of organic farming's superiority, there has been a growing discontent in this country towards organic and an increased push towards buying locally and regionally. Referenced as the "local foods" movement, with adherents often calling themselves "locavores," a term coined by Bay Area resident Jessica Prentice for World Environment Day 2005, the aims of the movement are to promote the practice of eating a diet consisting of food harvested from within a 100 mile radius of where one lives. The movement was born out of the realization that, for example, although most Americans live within 60 miles of an apple orchard, the apples they buy have traveled, on average, more than 1700 miles from the orchard, or that the typical carrot travels some 1838 miles to reach a dinner table—statistics that seem needlessly wasteful regardless of the method used to grow the produce.[42]

The local food movement is also a reaction to the rise of "Big Organic." In the early days of the organic movement, practitioners were generally small scale farms who sold their agriculturally products locally (within approximately 100 miles or so) and regionally (within roughly 400 miles). As the market for organic products increased, however, so too did the scale of the producers. Earthbound Farm Organic, for example, began a quarter of a century ago in someone's backyard and is now a collective of 150 farms spanning as much as 680 acres and shipping produce as far as 3000 miles away.[43] In addition to the massive growth of once small scale organic producers, the same agribusiness corporations that helped to usher in industrial agriculture have been increasingly infiltrating the organic agriculture movement. As just a few examples out of many, organic, fair trade, chocolate purveyor Green & Blacks was purchased by Cadbury, the second largest candy company in the world; pasta sauce and salad dressing company Seeds of Change was purchased by M&M Mars; General Mills purchased Cascadian Farm and Muir Glen; and The Organic Cow of Vermont was purchased by Dean Foods, a company notorious for slyly changing its Silk brand soymilk (which it purchased in 2002) from organic to conventional without so much as changing the product's UPC code, foisting it on unsuspecting consumers.

While the locavore movement initially tapped into a desire to connect with local farmers that frequented places such as community farmers' markets, increasingly the movement has become more about the determination of an urbanized populace to bring agriculture as close as to where they live as possible—namely, into the cities that more than 60 percent of Americans call home. Thus, the movement quickly gave rise to an urban agricultural model, with the logic that it does not get more local than growing food right where people live. Based on this paradigm, in 2007, local activist and goat enthusiast Jennie Grant cajoled the Seattle city council to legalize backyard goats.[44] These miniature wonders, weighing between 50 and 100 pounds and standing some two feet tall, provide effortless lawn mowing, and though they eat only half as much as your standard goat, produce two-thirds as much milk. Similarly, New York City, which has always legalized chickens (roosters, however, are illegal because they crow), made beekeeping legal in 2010. Since 2001, when Added Value farm in Red Hook, Brooklyn first hauled several dozen tons of soil to create a garden on the site of what was once an asphalt football field, urban farming as an occupation and not merely a hobby has taken off in the city, as rooftop farms such as Eagle Street Farms (in Brooklyn) and Brooklyn Grange (in Queens) have assumed the heavy task of growing food locally.

This trend is happening in other cites as well. In Montreal, Lufa Farms turned an office rooftop into a 31,000 square foot greenhouse that grows fresh lettuce, tomatoes, cucumbers, bok choy, eggplants, and fresh herbs year round.[45] In Philadelphia, The Philadelphia Horticultural Society has transformed nearly 32,000 square feet of City Center into a Pop Up Garden featuring peppers, corn, and quinoa. The supermarket chain Whole Foods is even considering putting greenhouses atop some of its stores. Meanwhile websites such as The City Chicken (dedicated to helping beginners learn how to raise chickens in their backyard), and Urban Farming (dedicated to helping urban communities launch gardens and farms in cities) seem to sprout daily.

The problem with all of these endeavors is that local food, although it has numerous social benefits, is not in and of itself all that green. In fact, the supposed main benefit of local food—low transportation costs—is discounted when one takes into account that only 11 percent of the 8.1 metric tons of greenhouse gases that the average U.S. household generates comes from food consumption, with final delivery from producer to retailer contributing only 4 percent. By comparison, the agricultural and industrial practices that go into growing and harvesting food account for 83 percent of greenhouse gas emissions.[46] Furthermore, the most egregious elements of transporting food—salmon, for example, harvested in the Pacific Northwest, shipped to China for low-cost filleting, and then returned to the US—is not reflected on the label of the food package.[47] Thus we, the American consumer, have no way of knowing that, on its way to our dinner table, our frozen salmon took a detour to China on its way from a river in Oregon. In addition, produce shipped from further away may in fact be less energy intense than produce grown in a local, but heated, greenhouse.

This isn't to say that buying local can't be green. Rooftop farms, for example, make use of an otherwise unused space, and if properly implemented, can drastically slash the energy requirements of the building below. Green roofs, also known as living roofs, are roofs that have been partially or completely covered with vegetation, and have been consistently shown to reduce surface run off by absorbing rainwater. Each year, the city of New York's sewer system spews 30 billion gallons of raw sewage into nearby waterways, such as Brooklyn's Gowanus Canal, because the aging system is unable to handle the sheer volume of storm water combined with the city's liquid waste. Green roofs are a relatively low-cost way of mitigating the overflow problem by reducing the amount of water that reaches the sewers. In addition, they reduce the heating and cooling costs of buildings by helping to trap in heat in winter and by absorbing heat before it can reach the building in summer. This has the doubly positive effect of extending the life of a roof and reducing the "heat island effect," which is the term to used describe the fact that urban areas are often several degrees warmer (due to all of the concrete and heavy use of air conditioning) than nearby rural areas, resulting in increased summer energy demand, air pollution and increased greenhouse gas emissions.

Despite the benefits of some forms of urban farming, many other plans of bringing agriculture to the city—such as erecting large glass, greenhouse skyscrapers—though often aesthetically beautiful, are environmentally suspect, as the skyscrapers require significant energy both to erect and to maintain while also reducing a key element that makes a city sustainable, its density. The greenest cities are the ones whose population density allows people to walk, cycle, or use mass transit to get around. Using urban agriculture to fragment that landscape does more to harm a city's sustainability than it does to help it by simply reducing its food miles.

Ultimately, the main benefit to buying local lies not in its ecological footprint, but in its potential to upend a food system in which for every dollar spent on a loaf of bread, farmers are paid as much for their wheat (6 cents) as the end user who transforms that wheat into bread pays for packaging.[48] As Slow Food founder Carlo Petrini points out,

> A lot of folks take a condescending view of the local dimension. They say your products are too minor, too marginal, but the opposite is true. If you join together as one, you small-scale producers arguably form the biggest food multinational of all. The difference is that you don't produce standardization or pollution...or poverty. You produce wealth, diversity, exchange, preservation of memory, and progress. Here we have the values of the local economy.[49]

The ability to reduce poverty is one of the major benefits of purchasing local, ensuring that farmers receive a fair price for their products and that humanity as a whole can eat. It has been argued that our current system turns food into a commodity, in the process divorcing agriculture both from people's need for food and from the normal rules of supply and demand. By turning food into a tool of financial speculation, industrial agriculture creates artificial cycles of boom and bust, of feast and of famine. Eventually, the system busts for reasons not related to food availability, but rather due to speculation and policy changes. At the same time, the system removes people from the land so that most can't grow food for themselves. Often, due to industrial agriculture's emphasis on crop specialization, farmers themselves can't survive exclusively on what they grow. The final result is a system wherein those born during boom years can find themselves lacking access to food during bust years. To be clear, hunger of this nature is rarely if ever an issue of availability. In fact, worldwide, we produce more than enough food to feed everyone, and even during times of famine, food is often readily available. It is simply unavailable at a price the starving can pay. This is why industrial agriculture, which encompasses not only the methods of production but also the system of distribution, makes global hunger worse. Hunger is no longer a question of production, but rather of access.

Thus, while there are many reasons to buy local—improved transparency, supporting local farmers, sustaining community—the myopic focus on what we consume and how it's grown obscures an equally significant problem with the industrial agricultural system, something that organic, biodynamic, or even locally grown does little to upend: For a system and a nation that prides itself on efficiency, we have created a food system that involves a staggering amount of waste.

Food waste is defined by the EPA, as "any food substance, raw or cooked, which is discarded, or intended or required to be discarded. Food wastes are the organic residues generated by the handling, storage, sale, preparation, cooking, and serving of food."[50] After paper, food is the single largest source of municipal waste in the United States, and it's growing. In the 1970s, the United States wasted roughly 900 kilocalories of food per person, per day, or roughly half the number of calories that your average sized adult should eat on a daily basis. Today, we waste 36 percent more calories, to the tune of 1400 kilocalories per person, per day.[51] This is the same number of calories a moderately active six year-old should eat in a day. On average, your typical American household throws out enough calories everyday to feed two moderately active adults. In total, just shy of half of the food we grow, a whopping 40 percent of the food that we expend considerable energy to plant, fertilize, water, harvest, and transport, is never consumed—we simply throw it out.[52] It seems that the recognition that we must finish our supper because of all the starving children around the world has all but faded from our consciousness.

Never mind that the sheer volume of this waste, some 34 million tons of food, is happening in the same country, the United States, that as of 2009 was also home to 17 million food insecure households.[53] And unlike agricultural techniques, in which we can blame the producer for simply trying to make a quick buck, food waste lies almost exclusively in our hands. Farmers are often forced to throw out perfectly good produce because supermarkets won't purchase it due to "quality standards" that reject food items not perfect in shape or appearance mainly because we, the consumer, won't purchase tomatoes that have split (and then healed themselves), peaches with an insect bite, or an avocado that deviates from "standard size." Tristram Stuart writes in the *Worldwatch Institute's State of the World 2011* that,

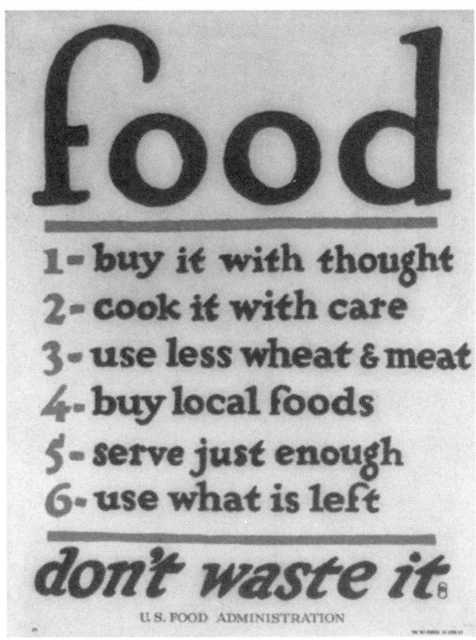

> the numerous tools that developed nations have at their disposal to prevent food from spoiling such as pasteurization, refrigerated transport units, and chemicals designed to expand shelf-life may ironically have contributed to the cornucopian abundance that has fostered a culture in which staggering levels of 'deliberate' food waste are now accepted or even institutionalized. Throwing away cosmetically 'imperfect' produce on farms, discarding edible fish at sea, over-ordering stock for supermarkets, and purchasing or cooking too much food in the home, are all examples of profligate negligence toward food.[54]

All too often, we take home our carefully screened produce, then allow that produce to spoil before we eat it. Roughly 42 percent of the food wasted in the US is on the consumer end—we simply throw out perfectly good food. The reason for this is that many of us can financially afford to waste food.[55] Every year, industrialized nations throw out 222 million tons of food, a mere three and a half percent less than the 230 million tons of food that sub-Saharan Africa produces in a year. That 43 million people in the United States suffer from periodic uncertainty as to the source of their next meal in the same country where on average we throw out nearly as much food as we eat, is not only morally reprehensible and illustrative of how far we've intelligently and emotionally separated food from the labor it takes to produce it, but also staggering in the scale of its ecological cost.[56]

Over the course of its production, the food we waste consumes 300 million barrels of oil per year, representing four percent of the total US oil consumption as of 2009—or roughly as much oil as the US consumes in 16 days.[57] Twenty-one percent of our nation's freshwater supply is used to grow food that we simply throw out. Once in landfills, this food continues to cause environmental harm by decomposing and releasing an odious mix of

50-percent CO2 and 50-percent methane gas. Landfills are the largest human generated source of methane, a gas that has 25 times the effect on climate change as carbon dioxide. According to the U.S. Energy Information Administration, in 2008, landfills generated the equivalent 184.3 million metric tons of carbon dioxide emissions in the form of methane gas.[58]

There is something uniquely beautiful about seeing food grow. A well tended fruit and vegetable garden, an apple orchard, a diverse old fashioned farm, all somehow evoke the beauty of the Luxembourg gardens or Hokusai's Great Wave, with the added benefit that we are able to eat the art. At the New York Botanical Garden's Family Garden, an agricultural garden nestled in the middle of a traditional Botanical Garden in the Bronx, staffers routinely have to stop the public from plucking and eating the fruits of their labor. When they actually see food being grown, children, whose parents have to beg, plead and cajole them into eating a single green bean, are somehow compelled to eat an unwashed, uncooked kale leaf or a vine ripened sun gold cherry tomato as though it was candy.

This points to the fact that there is something contradictorily primal yet civilized about understanding on both a visceral and intellectual level where one's food comes from. For example, when I was in graduate school, a handful of students hailing from Cameroon and Ethiopia would gather together, head to a local farm and alternatively kill a goat or a sheep before commencing to cook every last piece of it in a delicious melding of New England potluck culture and sub-Saharan African cuisines. The rest of us would provide the sides. Somehow understanding the full process of where the food came from, mingled with the outdoor air, made eating all the better. All the more connected.

Unfortunately, most of us today are completely divorced

from this process. It makes, then a certain kind of perverse sense then that when we enter the landscape of sustainable food, our understanding would be equally disjointed. And this disconnect allows most of us to ignore the fact that conventional agricultural techniques, which include a heavy reliance on artificial pesticides, fertilizers, and herbicides, though allowing us to bolster our agricultural production in the short term, have done so at a tremendous cost to both the ecological and human health of the planet. In addition, our use of genetically modified technologies to breach the void left by conventional technology have at best had no effect and at worst only hastened the spread of resistant species while extracting a significant human and environmental cost.

Into this void has stepped organic agriculture, which eschews both genetically modified and conventional agriculture techniques for methodologies that are lighter on the planet and healthier to humans. Yet as organic agriculture has increasingly adopted industrial agricultural techniques in terms of scale and distribution, many of us have shifted from purchasing organic to purchasing local, under the belief that this somehow reduces our environmental impact. The truth is that although there are many social (and culinary) benefits to purchasing foods grown locally, the reality is that transportation has only a negligible impact on agriculture's effect on the environment.

Far less compelling, but perhaps far more significant, is the sheer volume of our consumption. The easiest route to slashing the effects that agriculture has on the environment is simply to consume less. For those of us who live in the developed nations such as the United States, Canada and Western Europe, this doesn't actually mean eating less. Given the fact that roughly 40 percent of the food we grow is thrown out, it seems that the simplest way of reducing the environmental impact associated with the food we consume is to reduce the amount we waste. From accepting "ugly" fruit that may have been nibbled on by an insect or two, to simply cooking the food we bring home before it rots, reducing waste is the greenest thing that we can do as related to agriculture. Ensuring that we eat the peas that we purchase may be less sexy than offering your guest the latest bottle of biodynamic wine to accompany your locally grown, grass fed steak, but when it comes to food, that is truly what it means to eat "green."

3. HOW GREEN IS CLEAN?

Cosmetics are a boon to every woman, but a girl's best beauty aid is still a near-sighted man.—Yoko Ono

For the past few years, celebrities like Halle Berry, Lindsay Lohan, Reese Witherspoon and Salma Hayek have credited their smooth locks to a keratin based straightening process commonly referred to as the Brazilian Blowout, named for the company which first popularized the procedure in the United States. Positioned as a more natural, gentler-on-the-hair alternative to straightening curly locks and smoothing frizzy hair, thousands have flocked to salons and paid upwards of 250 dollars for the procedure, which lasts for approximately three months. The process entails washing the hair, toweling it dry, adding the keratin solution, blowing it straight, and then flat ironing the hair at a temperature of 450 degrees to lock in the treatment.

However, there was one significant problem with all of this. Many customers and stylists found that the fumes that escaped over the course of the process—most acutely during the drying and flat ironing stages—were irritating to the eyes and causing labored breathing. A 2007 expose article in, of all places, the beauty magazine *Allure*, in which the publication sent salon samples of the hair smoothing solution to independent, FDA registered labs, uncovered that most types of the formulation, sold under several different names in the US, including Marcia Teixeira Brazilian

Keratin Treatment, Advanced Keratin Treatment and Agi Maxx, contained the naturally occurring toxin formaldehyde at levels significantly higher than deemed healthy.[1] In addition to causing respiratory distress, formaldehyde, best known for its use in embalming fluid, is a known human carcinogen conclusively linked to respiratory cancers and possibly even leukemia. It was also the culprit behind the illnesses linked to the Hurricane Katrina FEMA trailers. Almost as soon as residents moved into the trailers, designed to provide temporary housing to those left homeless by the hurricane, they began to suffer health problems ranging from headaches and runny noses to chronic respiratory problems and nosebleeds. In addition, local pediatricians saw an uptick in children with persistent colds, and invariably, those children were living in FEMA trailers. When the Sierra Club tested the air quality of 44 FEMA trailers in Mississippi, 40 of them had formaldehyde concentrations at levels approaching what a professional embalmer would be exposed to on the job—and at least an embalmer is given safety equipment.[2]

When the formaldehyde-keratin blowout problem was leaked in 2007, many of the companies went back, reformulated their products, and returned with solutions labeled "formaldehyde free." This should have been the end of the issue. However, in September 2010, motivated by complaints from stylists, Oregon's Occupational Safety and Health Administration (OSHA), in conjunction with Oregon Health & Science University, released two separate reports detailing their chemical analysis of the formaldehyde concentrations of two supposedly formaldehyde-free Brazilian keratin hair straightening solutions—Acai Professional Smoothing Solution and Brazilian Blowout Solution. The products tested had an average formaldehyde rate of 9.5 percent and 4.8 percent, respectively.[3] For some context, if a product contains more than 0.1 percent formaldehyde, OSHA requires that the manufacturer list the formaldehyde on its material safety data sheet, to allow users of the product to take adequate protection measures. These hair care products had 95 and 48 times more the legal disclosure limit of formaldehyde, yet where labeled as formaldehyde free.

In one way, these labels were accurate, as strictly speaking, the Brazilian Blowout did not contain formaldehyde but instead methylene glycol. However, methylene glycol readily converts into formaldehyde when water is removed. Not surprisingly, blow drying and flat ironing solution-saturated hair removes water from the solution, converting it into formaldehyde. When pressed on this issue, however, Brazilian Blowout argued that since technically methylene glycol is not formaldehyde, their products were formaldehyde free—even though following the company's own directions for use created and thus exposed users to formaldehyde.[4] This is the argument that Brazilian Blowout used to file suit against Oregon's OSHA in 2010, arguing that that their studies, by measuring methylene glycol in its results, mislead consumers. This is not an argument that sat well with many of the users of the product, who filed a class action suit filed against the company for claiming that the product was free of formaldehyde. On the strength of these assurances stylists applied the product without gloves or masks, harming stylists, consumers, and the reputation of the salons that offered the service. Despite their claims that their product was formaldehyde-free, in 2011 Brazilian Blowout released a new version of the solution—Brazilian Blowout Zero—which is in fact formaldehyde and methlyene glycol free.

The situation with Brazilian Blowout is more than the typical company seeking to profit regardless of the long-term effects of its products on its consumers, akin to big tobacco hiding the health effects of cigarettes; it's actually scarier and more insidious. In the strictest definition of the truth, the keratin treatment products were clearly labeled with what they actually contained, ostensibly designed to inform the consumer. However, most of these products were designed to be sold to salons only—thus customers rarely if ever saw the labels. And even if they had seen the labels, the list of ingredients on the back of cosmetics are often so technical and complicated that unless said consumer is also armed with an advanced degree in organic chemistry, she'd be hard pressed to make heads or tails of it. After all, how many people know that methylene glycol breaks down into formaldehyde when water is removed? Cosmetics labels are so rich with the language of chemists that it's almost impossible for the layperson to understand which products pose a potential health risk and which ones do not. Government regulation makes it even harder by allowing seemingly innocuous and straightforward words such as "fragrance" and "natural" to mask an additional—sometimes toxic—list of ingredients.

As an example, I've reproduced the label from *King of Shaves for Men Antibacterial Alpha Shave Gel* that is, upon close examination, loaded with the kinds of ingredients one would be hard pressed to coat themselves with knowingly. Propylene glycol, for example, better known as anti-freeze, is used in a variety of cosmetics, including liquid foundation makeup and deodorant, to provide moisture and to keep products from melting in high heat and freezing in the cold (the same reason we pump it into car

Aqua/Water/Eau, Aloe Vera (Aloe Barbadensis) Leaf Juice, Sodium Laureth Sulfate, Acrylates/C10 30 Alkyl Acrylate Crosspolymer, Melaleuca Altemifolia (Tea Tree) Leaf Oil, Glycerin, Triethanolamine, Cocamidopropyl Betaine, Polyacrylamide, Sodium Chloride, Triclosan, Benzophenone 4, Citric Acid, Salix Nigra (Willow Bark) Extract, Magnesium Nitrate, Sodium Benzoate, Benzyl Alcohol, Camellia Sinensis (Green Tea) Leaf Extract, Cinnamomum Camphora (Camphor) Bark Oil, Propylene Glycol, Potassium Sorbate, Magnesium Chloride, Methylchloroisothiazolinone, methylisothiazolinone, Methylparaben, Sorbic Acid (A Preservative), Limonene, CI 42090 (Blue 1), Yellow 5 (CI 19140)

Ingredient list for King of Shaves For Men Antibacterial Alpha Shave Gel

engines). Ironically, it is actually one of the safer chemicals that appear in our cosmetics.

Sodium Lauryl (SLS)/Laureth Sulfate (SLES) are common ingredients found in toothpastes, shampoos and soaps. They are what give shampoo its lather and what enables toothpaste to foam—which are ultimately what many of us associate with the concept of "clean." Contrary to popular perception, however, although SLS/SLES may strip your hair of essential oils (which is why people who dye their hair are told to avoid shampoos and conditioners that contain SLS/SLES), there isn't sufficient evidence to indicate that they cause cancer. They are, however, a known skin irritant and their use is associated with the development of skin related problems such as contact dermatitis.[5] A fact that is even still more ironic when one considers that products such as Dove's Sensitive Skin Nourishing Body Wash—which, true to its name, promises to "nourish" the skin—contains sodium laureth sulfate. Similarly, the presence of sodium lauryl and sodium laureth sulfate in toothpaste has been known to trigger canker sores in predisposed individuals.

The chemical compound methylparaben belongs to a class of chemicals known as parabens that are often used as preservatives in cosmetics because they kill off bacteria and fungi. They also have the dubious distinction of being a chemical found not only in the usual places—shampoos, moisturizes, shaving gels, spray tans, sunscreen products, lipsticks, and toothpaste—but also in food, often hidden in breakfast cereal, bread, and processed foods under the ambiguous title of "preservatives." This wouldn't be the problem if parabens weren't so structurally similar to estrogen that they disrupt our body's own internal hormonal balance, causing early puberty in girls and testicular enlargement and breast development in young boys.[6] Parabens have also been implicated in helping breast cancer grow—an Environmental Working Group study found that 19 out of 20 breast cancer tumors contained parabens—and in lowering the sperm count in men.[7] Methylparaben has also been shown to age the skin—ironic given the fact that it's often placed into products that claim anti-aging effects.[8]

Even worse, parabens along with cinnamate, benzophenone, and camphor derivatives—key ingredients in commonly used sunscreens—have been found to cause the bleaching, or death, of coral reefs. With bold blues, vibrant pinks, and of course, psychedelic corals, coral reefs are among the world's most biologically productive and diverse ecosystems. Tragically, roughly sixty percent of the world's coral reefs are currently threatened with extinction. And yet, every day, when millions of beachgoers dutifully slather on sun block to protect themselves from the sun's rays, they are at the same time contributing to the death of these critical ecosystems.[9]

Parabens are not the only commonly used personal care product ingredient that is threatening marine habitats. Triclosan, an antibacterial and antifungal agent that was originally developed in the 1970s as a surgical scrub, has spread far beyond the operating room, as its ubiquitous presence is now seen in liquid hand soaps, body soaps, shaving gels, and even, oddly, in dish washing liquid. Yet the same properties that make it so successful at keeping bacteria at bay—namely that it kills things—render it harmful to the larger environment. Studies have increasingly linked triclosan to a number of health and environmental effects ranging from skin irritation to the dioxin contamination of delicate aquatic ecosystems.[10] In the ultimate boomerang effect, the triclosan that leaves our home when we wash our hands or hair or brush our teeth by trickling down our drains out to rivers, streams or the sea, converts upon exposure to the sun's ultraviolet light into dioxin. The dioxin then builds up in aquatic species, such as fish, which return to our home as dinner.

This cycle of life—the ultimate in recycling—wouldn't be problematic if dioxins were not so toxic. Perhaps you recall Victor Yushchenko, the 2004 Ukrainian presidential candidate and opposition leader, whose face was disfigured due to a mysterious disease during his presidential run? The mysterious disease was chloracne, an eruption of blackheads, cysts, boils and pustules that are a side effect of dioxin poisoning.[11] And chloracne is not the worst of dioxin's effects, which also include liver damage, diabetes, problems with thyroid functioning, diabetes and immune disorders. In children, dioxin negatively impacts sexual and tooth development. And as if that wasn't enough, dioxins also cause cancer.

Triclosan has other problems as well, as its widespread use in popular culture has hastened the speed with which pathogens have become immune not only to its effects but to a wider specter of antibiotics. And, by altering the kinds of bacteria—including the elimination of beneficial bacteria—that we have in our bodies, our use of triclosan may lead to an increase in autoimmune disorders such as allergies. Pointed out Massachusetts Congressman Edward Markey in 2010:

> The proliferation of triclosan in everyday consumer products is so enormous, it is literally in almost every type of product—most soaps, toothpaste, cosmetics, clothes and toys...It's in our drinking water, it's in our rivers and as a result, it's in our bodies.... I don't think a lot of additional data has to be collected in order to make the simple decisions about children's toys and soaps that people use. It clearly is something that creates a danger.[12]

And this is just the tip of the iceberg. According to the Environmental Working Group, a mere 10 percent of the 10,500 ingredients that the FDA says are currently in use in personal care products have been evaluated by a publicly accountable institution.[13] Even fewer have been tested to see what happens when they're applied together with other chemicals. Many chemicals that are thought to be safe when consumed alone may have nasty side effects when combined with other products. Think of the childhood experiment of making a volcano out of baking soda and vinegar. Alone each of the chemicals are harmless and inert; in combination they're explosive. While the aforementioned keratin based straightening products are toxic enough when simply applied to the hair, that's a risk that can easily be mitigated, at least on the stylist's end, by simply wearing gloves. The heat applied in the process, however, turns the formaldehyde into gas, increasing the likelihood of problems for the user. That we not only don't test our products individually, but also that fail to test how those products react when applied with other commonly used chemicals, at the same time that we happily coat ourselves with 10 to 12 personal care products daily, exposing ourselves to some 126 chemicals that cause harm to ourselves, to wildlife and to waterways, is worrisome. A growing number of studies have found our personal care product ingredients in rivers and streams across the country, including some whose ingredients have been linked to the feminization of fish and other aquatic life. [14]

Based on all this, it is no wonder that there is an increasing market for "natural" or "chemical free" personal care products. Among these are tried and true brands such as Burt's Bees (now owned by Clorox) and ninety year old personal care company Weleda, as well as a growing number of relative newcomers. Method, for example, which first came to the market in 2000 selling eco-friendly housecleaning products in stylish containers, now sells hand sanitizers and body wash along with glass and toilet cleaner. Meanwhile, the distinctly homey Badger brand of personal care products was first whipped up in 1995 in the kitchen of Bill and Katie Whyte, which is likely why their products rely heavily on an impressive list of easily recognizable ingredients such as olive oil, castor oil, and beeswax.

But the question remains: How green are these products? The answer is, "it depends." No other consumption category, except for perhaps food, is as fraught with as many potential landmines as are personal care products. The problem is that "green" is not an industry defined term—there is no standard to which a company must aspire in order to achieve sustainability. In practice, this means companies can simply list their claims and consumers are left trying to figure out what are the best "green" products to use. Thus, Tom's of Maine (now majority owned by Colgate-Palmolive), a company which proudly declares that it doesn't test on animals, eschews artificial colors, flavors, fragrances, and preservatives, maximizes recycled content and recyclability, and emphasizes transparency by sharing every ingredient, its purpose and its source on its website, and whose labels include mostly easy to identify ingredients, uses SLS in its products. Occupying the same market niche is Jason's Natural (now owned by Hain Celestial), which says that its products contain "unique formulations infused with botanicals," though the ingredient list on their toothpaste is significantly longer than that of Tom's, and therefore harder to understand. However, it is SLS free. Ultimately, the consumer is left to choose what product to buy based on what is most in their own interest, not what best suits the planet—because it's hard to tell which is better, if any are.

Similarly, consider L'Oreal's EverPure line of hair care products. The name EverPure is clearly designed to evoke purity, and the brand's bottles boast in very big letters that not only is it sulfate free but also made with "natural botanicals" and is "100 percent vegan." This makes it seem like it might be green until you realize that EverPure products contain not only methlylparaben but also butylphenyl methylpropional—an artificial fragrance whose use has been banned in many countries, including the European Union.

Speaking of fragrance, have you ever noticed that many products won't list their actual scents and just hide behind the generic term "fragrance." This is because companies are not obligated to list the chemicals that go into their fragrance, pushing the idea that their fragrance recipes are proprietary secrets and that divulging them would give competitors an unfair advantage.

However, "fragrances" are often a source of parabens. This is the problem with labels that define themselves less by what they contain and more by what they don't. By informing us, for example, that a product comes in BPA free packaging or that, as in the case of Loreal EverPure, that it is SLS free, most of us feel that the product is relatively safe. However, that often isn't the case.

And then of course there's the problem of genuine greenwashing, where companies simply make unsubstantiated claims on their packages. For example, knowledgeable shoppers know that the word "natural" on a label means nothing, and that "organic" without the USDA Certified logo as well as some kind of information regarding how much of the product is organic means that the product is likely anything but organic. Unfortunately, many shoppers are not that savvy and get suckered in by false claims. In June 2011, a lawsuit filed by the California based Center for Environmental Health revealed that dozens of personal care products such as shampoos, lotions, toothpastes were deliberately mislabeled as organic despite containing little to no organic ingredients, in violation of California state law. Several of the products—including some meant for children—contained the same toxic chemicals included in conventional products that are suspected of causing respiratory problems such as asthma, disrupting hormones, and causing cancer, amongst other health problems. In a public statement, Michael Green the executive Director of CEH, said

> For years, organic advocates have called on personal care companies to fix their improper 'organic' labels, but our recent purchasing shows the industry is still rife with unsubstantiated organic claims. We want to encourage companies to use organic ingredients, and insure that consumers can trust organic labels to be meaningful and consistent.[15]

The reason for this all confusion and misrepresentation is that the $50 billion dollar personal care industry is largely unregulated. The law that currently governs the industry—the Food, Drug and Cosmetics Act of 1938—hasn't been significantly updated since its inception, which is why an industry that uses more than 12,5000 chemical ingredients is given the latitude to put products on the shelves without prior FDA approval. Companies also don't have to notify the FDA about adverse reactions, which is how L'Oreal, a French company, can get away with putting a chemical it knows is harmful in its EverPure line even as it pulls that product from use in Europe. Unless someone knows that something is problematic and raises enough attention to get it tested, consumers are in the dark. This is why getting triclosan's use regulated has been a nightmare, as its regulation is overseen by three different government agencies.

This isn't to say that we can't trust any labels. The ingredient list for Badger Balms Cuticle Care, for example—Shea Butter, Extra Virgin Olive Oil, Castor Oil, Beeswax, Essential Oils of Geranium Mandarin, Lemongrass, Cardamom, Rosemary Verbenone, Litsea, and CO2 Extracts of Seabuckthorn Berry, & Ginger—seems unlikely to be harmful, partially because many of the ingredients are readily identifiable, but also because it's devoid of vague terms such as "fragrance" or "natural flavors." It's just important to keep in mind that no one's really checking to make sure that these claims are true.

There is however a larger question—just because something isn't toxic does not mean that product is sustainable. For example, can a body lotion whose main ingredient is palm oil harvested from a plantation in Southeast Asia on clear cut forest land be considered sustainable? It may not hurt marine life, but I doubt the proboscis monkey whose life is threatened by such incursions would find much solace in this fact. Similarly, while the attention on what goes into personal care products tends to focus on the belief that if they're harmful to our bodies they can't possibly be beneficial to the earth, in being so narrowly focused we fail to give adequate attention to the environmental cost of bringing these products—even "green" products—from the field, the factory and the store to our home. While some companies have given some thought to what happens at the end of a products' lifecycle, with companies such as Aveda selling their products in refillable containers and Garnier partnering with green manufacturing company Terracycle to recycle their products into garbage cans, benches and other plastic goods, the reality is that product packaging represents the highest environmental footprint for the health and beauty industry, and is also a significant contributor to landfills. As Allen Hershkowitz, a senior scientist at the Natural Resources Defense Council (NRDC) said in a 2007 *Time Magazine* article,

> There have been some noble efforts, but it's not the disposal of the plastic container that causes the big environmental impact. It's the production of the bottle. The coal, the gas, the coloring agents, the heavy-metal stabilizers, the refining of the petroleum to make the plastic containers—it all creates a tremendous amount of toxic air emissions.[16]

Ultimately, when it comes to personal care products, the greenest thing that most of us can do is to purchase products from companies who use the fewest, easiest to understand ingredients and have the greatest transparency. We can do this by finding producers who are focused on greening their product sources, their manufacturing facilities, and their packaging. At the same time, we can also drastically reduce the ecological impact of our need to be clean and sweet smelling by simply reducing the number of products that we use. Most of use at least a dozen personal care products when in many cases half as many would easily do (there are few of us, after all, who would feel comfortable going without toothpaste). From the chemicals that go into a product, to the package, to the effort it takes to manufacture and ship those products, each step in the chain contributes to an ever growing list of harm to humans and the planet. The easiest thing to do, the greenest thing, is to simply use less of whatever we are using.

4. THE GREEN CAR MYTH: THINKING BEYOND THE TAIL PIPE

It wasn't the Exxon Valdez captain's driving that caused the Alaskan oil spill. It was yours. —Greenpeace Advertisement

Americans are broad-minded people. They'll accept the fact that a person can be an alcoholic, a dope fiend, a wife beater, and even a newspaperman, but if a man doesn't drive, there is something wrong with him.—Art Buchwald

Forget the damned motor car and build the cities for lovers and friends.—Lewis Mumford

On a dusty road off Route 16 in the tiny southern Massachusetts town of Mendon, amidst a forest of white pine and eastern hemlock, red maple and paper birch, tower two large movie screens. Here, in a field by the side of the road, it is still possible to catch a screening of the latest blockbuster film for less than the cost of a meal at the local McDonalds, as Mendon is home to one of the ever dwindling number of drive-in movie theaters in the United States.

The drive-in, getting one's kicks on Route 66, Kerouac's *On the Road*, and, more contemporarily, drive-thru restaurants, pharmacies, banks and even drive-thru liquor stores, are all heavily intertwined with an important ideal of what it is to be an American—namely, to drive. As Uruguayan journalist Eduardo Galeano notes, "A driver's license is required to pay by check to cash a check, to sign for most documents or to notarize a contract. A driver's license is the most common ID: cars give people their identity."[1] It is an identity that relishes the open road and to which a car isn't merely a method of getting from point A to point B, but a symbol of freedom. Says Calli Khouri, Oscar-winning screenwriter of *Thelma & Louise*, "To everyone in this country, the car represents freedom, mobility, and the control you feel over your destiny/destination."[2] Cars, we are told, are hall passes to freedom, or to what author James Kunstler calls the "liberation from the daily bondage of place."[3]

Never mind that, on average, Americans spend 36 hours a year not zipping through empty highways or on back country adventures as advertised in car commercials, but stuck in traffic, staring at someone else's freedom loving tail pipe. In addition, 3.5 million Americans spend more than three hours a day driving to and from work, the equivalent of spending one month of their lives on the road each year. The reality is that for all this talk of freedom, what cars seem to do best is to keep us tethered to highways and to jobs that 55 percent of us, according to recent studies, hate.[4] After housing costs, the bulk of the American household budget goes to owning and maintaining cars. According to 2009 Bureau of Labor Statistics numbers, the average American spends 33 percent of their income on their home and 20 percent of their income on their cars.[5] This is more than we spend on food (13 percent) and healthcare (6 percent) combined, and stands in stark contrast to what we pay for education (2 percent). And yet most of us can't imagine a life, a reality, without the passenger car.

This cognitively dissonant love affair with the automobile isn't merely cultural—it's also structural. From the 1920's through the 1950's Standard Oil, Phillips Petroleum (now ConocoPhillips), General Motors and Firestone Tire colluded in what's now known as the "the great American streetcar scandal" to purchase and then dismantle street car and railroad systems throughout the United States. They did so not because they felt that the American people would be better served by the passenger car, but rather to increase their own corporate bottom lines. By replacing trolleys with passenger cars, General Motors sold more cars, Firestone more tires, and Standard Oil and Phillips Petroleum more gas. To fatten the wallets of a handful of industrialists, we completely transformed the landscape of America from one of dense, urban centers surrounded by farmland, to a nation in which cities are surrounded by suburbs and even more distant exurbs. Many of these newer suburbs lack sidewalks, rendering cars the only functional way of getting around. This transformed America from a nation where 90 percent of its citizens relied on mass transit to one where 90 percent of its population now drives to work. Only a mere 5 percent of us commute to work by mass transit, and a paltry 3 percent of us walk.[6]

Today, the United States, home to some 307 million people, has 210 million licensed drivers and some 246 million registered automobiles, which comes to 1.2 cars for every registered driver.[7] We have more cars on the road than any other country in the world; even China with its more than one billion people barely tips the scales at 170 million cars. The United States has roughly 800 cars for every thousand people—including the 70 or so million who are too young, too old, too ill (such as epileptics) or are legally blind, and thus can't drive. China, by contrast, has a mere 128 cars for every thousand people. On both an absolute and a per capita basis, we have more cars than any other country in the world. And, not only do we have more cars, but they pollute more than those of other nations as well. Although we are just 3 percent of the world's population, we own 30 percent of the world's cars, which account for 45 percent of global automotive greenhouse gas emissions.[8]

Yet, even as we choke on the detritus of automobile culture, the public discussion rarely questions the supremacy of cars as our principal form of transit. On the contrary, with the exception of a few urban centers—most notably New York City, where less than half of all households own cars—mass transit is often dismissed as a European or Japanese ideal because, supposedly, the US doesn't have the population density to support an extensive transit system. However, Russia—the world's largest country by size—somehow manages to have a mere 213 cars per thousand inhabitants. Similarly, in Canada, with roughly a tenth of the population of the United States and a landmass that rivals our own sprawling nation, there are a mere 563 cars per 1000 inhabitants, roughly 25 percent fewer than in the US.

The only thing that has forced us take even a sidelong glance at our car culture is oil. Not the 93 people on average killed every day, the 34,000 people killed every year, in car accidents across the United States.[9] Not the additional 30,000 people who die every year from the noxious mix of nitrous oxides, lead, and cancer causing particulate matter that comprise car exhaust. Not the fact that the number of people that cars kill every year is equal to two times the population of Burlington, Vermont, or is roughly twenty-times the number of people killed in the Twin Towers on September 11. Only oil, with its ever unpredictable price at the pump and, even more importantly, its detrimental effects on the environment, has finally forced us to question our car habit...at least a little.

By now, most of us have become aware of the specter of climate change. The planet is getting warmer, which is causing rising sea levels, as well as shifting weather patterns, reducing rainfall in some places, while causing too much in other places, which leads to increased flooding, droughts, crop loss, and a host of other problems that while horrific in theory are even worse in reality. Human activity—specifically the release of too much carbon dioxide by burning oil, coal, natural gas, among other things—has trapped climate warming chemicals in our atmosphere. The result is a climate that is shifting in fundamental ways. Writes author and environmental activist Bill McKibben in a June/July 2008 *Orion* Magazine article,

> How do you say, the world you know today, the world you were born into, the world that has remained essentially the same for all of human civilization, that has birthed every play and poem and novel and essay, every painting and photograph, every invention and economy, every spiritual system (and every turn of phrase) is about to be . . . something so different?[10]

The scientific consensus is that we are already experiencing some climatic events. For example, the population of the low lying island of Kandholhudhoo, part of the island nation The Maldives, are considered by many as the leading edge of what will be a tidal wave of climate refugees. The island was completely decimated by the 2004 South Indian Ocean Tsunami and most of its inhabitants, fearing rising sea levels and worsening storms, are in the process of being relocated. The majority are being relocated to other islands within the Maldives, but with the nation itself standing just a hares breath above sea level, the future of the entire country is in jeopardy unless we drastically reduce the amount of carbon (and carbon equivalent) gasses that we pump into the atmosphere. The Maldives—a very small, relatively poor nation—has done almost nothing to contribute to global climate change. And yet our unwillingness to take the reins and radically shift our behavior has left them imperiled.

Much like a very large SUV takes quite awhile to stop even after its driver slams on the brakes, climate change's progress will continue even after—and if—we reduce the amount of carbon we place in the atmosphere. What we can do, however, is slow it down before horrific, wide scale, irreversible damage is done to ecosystems. Continuing in the language of cars, we may not be able to avoid hitting the passenger vehicle, but if we act now, and take significant steps—that is reducing the amount of carbon in the atmosphere from its current number of 390 parts-per-million or ppm, to 350 ppm—we can at least avoid hitting the school bus. For Americans, this means we have to change the way we drive. According to the United States Department of Energy, our car habit releases on average 1.7 billion tons of CO2 into the atmosphere every year.[11] In addition, cars make up 51 percent of the average household's greenhouse gas emissions.[12] Reducing the environmental impact of cars, would, conventional wisdom goes, mean increasing fuel efficiency.

It is into this dismal picture that the Toyota Prius stepped onto the scene. Introduced in the United States in 2001, the hybrid-electric Prius is powered by a mix of gas and electricity. Power is generated by harvesting the electric energy created when the car brakes. This unique engine set-up, in conjunction with an ergonomic design, allowed drivers to get an estimated 41 miles per gallon (2012 models allow drivers to get roughly 50 miles per gallon), or roughly 50 percent more miles per gallon than the average passenger car. The Prius was the first commercially successful hybrid electric vehicle introduced to the US market. (Its predecessor, the Honda Insight, though more fuel efficient, was a commercial flop.)

Toyota's early pitch for the car—with taglines such as "'you don't have to plug it in" and "When it sees red...it charges," in conjunction with the company's heavy use of celebrity product placement (they shuttled "green" celebs to award shows in Prius vehicles instead of limos)—showed that the eco-friendly nature of the Prius was not its initial selling point. Instead, the car was positioned to sell to tech obsessed early adopters and image obsessed *Lifestyles of Health and Sustainability*, or LOHAS, the acronym bequeathed to the market segment concerned with health and fitness, the environment, personal development, sustainable living, and social justice, but only as far as it extends to their shopping cart. A 2007 research report by the marketing firm CNW concluded that customers choose the Prius over similar alternatives such as the hybrid version of the Honda Civic because the Prius is exclusively, identifiably a hybrid. Only 36 percent cited fuel economy as the motivator for buying a Prius, while 57 percent said their primary reason was that it "makes a statement about me."[13] In other words, they cared less about being green, than about *appearing* green, a supposition backed in research by economists Steven and Alison Sexton, who found that many LOHAS were willing to spend a premium of several thousand dollars to signal their environmental credibility through their choice of vehicle, an effect they termed the "green halo."[14]

In choosing to cater to the LOHAS, in addition to being profitable—the Prius outperforms all its competitors in the US—Toyota managed to tap in and reinforce a vein of thinking that frames sustainability as a personal, lifestyle choice that can somehow coexist in an uneasy alliance with its environmentally toxic brethren.[15] This idea individualizes sustainability, and ignores that on many levels sustainability—or lack thereof—is an outcome of how human systems—in this case transportation systems—function, and that our individual actions are influenced by those systems, in the process, distracting us from the very real work of saving the planet. In this way, Toyota managed to tap into the historical manner in which cars were initially conceived and marketed. Write Dutch clinical psychologists René Diekstra and Martin Kroon:

> The automobile culture was born among the upper classes—the nobility, bankers, manufacturers, theatre stars and prominent academics. The rich demonstrated to the astounded masses what the motor car signified: social status, freedom, and independence, and—above all—an opportunity to escape from the crowd. From the early years of the automobile, the belief that the car is a symbol of social superiority and individuality became embedded in the soul of elite and mass alike. ..Many car drivers still consider themselves superior to those who use a less powerful form of transport or a less powerful

> type of car...Once behind the wheel of a car, the driver is often—for himself and for others—no longer just the 'man in the street'. He demands and is given priority, which implies superiority and sets him apart from cyclists and pedestrians.[16]

The Prius specifically, and hybrid vehicles in general, do nothing to upend this illusion of a car as more than just transportation, but of freedom, of good taste, of general superiority, an attitude that is rampant across the automobile market. By 2011, the natural gas fueled Honda Civic GX, and another dozen or vehicles had joined the Prius in the "green" car market. Even General Motors joined in the game, rolling out a hybrid version of its full-sized Silverado pickup truck that though it has a hybrid engine, gets a laughable 21 miles to the gallon.

The car that was, however, the most seductive in connecting with the idea of alternative automobile superiority, is the new, completely electric Nissan Leaf. The commercial for the Leaf opens on a polar bear watching its arctic home melt away. The polar bear then proceeds to travel an arduous journey across tundra, through forests, under highway overpasses, across tractor trailer filled roads, and over bridges to hug a suburban businessman for purchasing a Leaf. The ad closes with a shot of the logo and a voice over announcing "The one hundred percent electric Nissan Leaf, innovation for the planet, innovation for all." Who wouldn't feel environmentally superior purchasing a polar bear approved vehicle?

Yet we need to upend this illusion if we want to get everyone thinking holistically about transportation. Although on the surface these alternatives seem green, too often they aren't. If what makes cars unsustainable is that they simply consume too much gas, logic would dictate that reducing their gas consumption would be at least a step in the right direction. The truth is not so simple. First, the problem with these "fuel efficient" vehicles is that many drivers erode the fuel efficiency gains of the vehicle by simply driving more. Why that happens is complicated. Hybrid drivers may very well purchase their vehicles because they drive a lot and want the most fuel efficient car they can get. Or, it could be that how much people drive, and the fuel efficiency of the cars they choose to drive, are tied to how much gas costs. As gas prices increase, people do drive less, but if gas prices continue to remain high, they buy more fuel efficient cars. Since driving a Prius effectively makes the cost per mile of a gallon of gas cheaper, Prius owners drive more. This idea, known in economics as Jevons Paradox, is the theory that technological change that increases the efficiency of use of a resource tends to, paradoxically, increase the rate of use of that resource. From 2001, when the Prius was first introduced, to 2007, the amount of fuel consumed by passenger vehicles increased by over 7 percent. [17] It wasn't until the economic crisis of 2008 that American consumption declined. Similarly, from 2001 through 2009 the last year for which the Bureau of Transportation Statistics has numbers, the fuel efficiency of light passenger cars has moved from 22.1 miles per gallon to 22.6 miles per gallon. This 2.3 percent increase is below the 85 percent reduction in total emissions that we need to stave off global warming. Efficiency may have increased, but so too did consumption.

Further, because hybrid cars get their electrical energy from braking, they are at their most fuel efficient in cities where stop signs and red lights make braking a routine action. Hybrid cars are less efficient on highways. Similarly, electric cars, since they can only go but so far on a single charge, also work best in cities. Cities, however, are places where population densities can easily support the far greener alternatives of mass transit, bicycling, or, simply walking. In other words, the best places for hybrid and electric cars are places where they supplant greener alternatives.

Ultimately, all this talk of fuel efficiency obscures a significant point: even if we could get cars to run on hydrogen, or water, or pixie dust, the individual passenger car as the principal form of transport for the ten billion people who will call this planet home by 2100 can never be sustainable. And the emissions, or tail pipe, issue is only the tip of the iceberg of what makes the automobile unsustainable. Think for a moment about the tremendous amount of energy it takes to manufacture a car in the first place. Extracting the raw material, transporting those materials, turning them into finished parts, assembling the car, all takes a large amount of resources and energy. For example, your typical car is more than 80 percent metal, so on average it takes a ton of steel to build a car, two tons to build a truck. Each ton of steel releases roughly two tons of green house gasses. Studies have shown that the energy it takes to make a car, known as the embodied energy, amounts to between fifteen percent and twenty-two percent of all of the energy consumed over the life of the car.[18] Even if we could get the driving emissions down to zero, the process of manufacturing cars would still emit a tremendous amount of greenhouse gasses. The best way of driving down this energy cost is to first build highly fuel efficient cars, and secondly to drive them for much longer than the standard eight years the average American currently keeps their car. As a 2008 *Wired* Magazine article points out, buying, in 2010, a used, highly efficient car from the early 90's can be as green as or even greener than purchasing a brand new hybrid.[19] Says author Matt Powers "Get behind the wheel of a 1994 Geo Metro , which matches the (2008) Prius' 46 mpg, and the Prius would never close the carbon gap."[20]

There are two things that a 1994 Geo Metro is not. Safe, for one, as over the intervening eighteen years since the Geo rolled off the Suzuki production line there have been a number of automobile safety improvements that would make the National Highway Traffic Safety Administration (NHTSA) shudder at the thought of legions of Americans giving up their newer cars for old Geo's. Fortunately for the NHTSA, that isn't likely to happen, because the other thing that the 1994 Geo Metro is not is sexy, as the car's squat, rounded form is more reminiscent of a gremlin than a jaguar. But, overall, this is an excellent illustration of just how, complicated the current energy picture is, as the problem with the concept of a "green" vehicle extends far beyond the car itself.

For example, anyone who has spent some time in a developing nation or in the back country knows that what makes car transport possible is not just the car, but the existence of well paved roads. Zooming across town at 100 miles an hour in a Prius, as Al Gore's son allegedly did in 2007 on a San Diego freeway, would be impossible on a Vermont dirt road during mud season.[21] The problem is that the modern roadway, regardless of what you're driving, is not green. The construction of one single mile, of one single lane, of a highway's smooth, perfectly paved road surface consumes between 7,000 and, 12,000 tons of raw materials—the same amount used by 600 to 1,000 US households annually.[22] In the process, that same tiny mile emits some 500 to 1,200 tons of carbon dioxide. The original two-lane Route 66, which spanned some 2,448 miles from Chicago to Los Angeles, would have consumed some 342,720,000 tons of raw materials in its construction, and emitted roughly 2.5 million tons of greenhouse gasses. And none of these numbers include the amount of raw materials and greenhouse gasses used to maintain these roads once they're built. A study referenced in the September 2005 issue of the *Journal of Urban Planning and Development* estimates that building and maintaining roads adds an additional 45 percent to the average car's annual climate footprint.[23]

And it's not just that cars are dependent on roads, but rather that car culture and the way it expands what is considered a reasonable distance to travel in a span of time perpetuates the continued need for ever more roads. Even in cities where populations are in decline, such as Buffalo and Detroit, road building is increasing as the suburban fringes expand outward. From 1960 through 2009, the United States added roughly half a million miles of public roads, bringing the national total to some four million miles of highways, byways, rural routes and city streets.[24] This expansion has been pushed by a growing population, an increasing percentage of drivers (more households in the 1960's owned but a single car), and by the rise of suburbs. As people have pushed further and further away from the urban core, we have built more roads leading from cities to the suburbs to the exurbs. Today, Peekskill New York, a sixty minute drive from New York City without traffic, is considered a commuting suburb.[25] However, the life that this car focused society has created is not sustainable, ecologically or sociologically. According to a 2005 *Businessweek* article detailed the life of these long distance drivers, known as "extreme commuters,"

> The costs of commuting—in gas, congestion, pollution, and sprawl—are high. Commuting is also associated with raised blood pressure, musculoskeletal disorders, increased hostility, lateness, absenteeism, and adverse effects on cognitive performance. Harvard University public policy professor Robert D. Putnam, author of Bowling Alone: The Collapse and Revival of American Community, says that for every 10 minutes of commuting time, one's social connections get cut by 10%. Imagine what that means when it's not a matter of minutes but hours.[26]

Similarly, a Swedish study has shown that married couples with at least one spouse who is a long distance commuter are more likely to divorce than couples with shorter commutes.[27]

In addition to their negative social effects, roads are also substantial ecological hazards. Increasing the number of roads makes cities hotter, setting temperatures soaring to levels higher than surrounding regions, the aforementioned heat island effect. This naturally leads many people to crank their air conditioning (an unintended side effect of road culture) which does much to increase our consumption of energy and little to help our changing climate. An increased number of paved surfaces also mean that water from rainstorms or from thawing snow isn't absorbed into the ground. Under normal circumstances, rain falls into the ground and is absorbed, in the process nourishing plant roots and contributing to the water cycle and other ecological processes. But when you pave over that land, it acts like a tarp, and the water isn't absorbed but rather rolls off. In cities, the water should be collected in storm drains and released after proper treatment. However, as cities have paved over more and more of their land to keep up with car culture, the drains and water sanitation systems have been unable to keep up. As a result, storm water systems frequently overflow, releasing untreated water into rivers and streams and increasing the likelihood of floods and landslides. Further, because roadways themselves are made from hazardous chemicals, when it rains the water absorbs these chemicals from their surfaces and drags these chemicals into nearby waterways and into surrounding soil sediment.

Roads also split up or fragment wildlife habitats by breaking up large patches of land into smaller ones, fundamentally changing landscapes that had been shaped by natural disturbances that species have adapted to over the millennia. This fragmentation process creates "edge" habitats along the sides of the roads, sometimes at the expensive of interior habitats. The kinds of wildlife that can exist along the sides of roads differ greatly from the kinds of animal life that exist in the interior. Edge habitats are often home to weedy, invasive, opportunistic species that under normal circumstances are kept in check by a myriad of other species. Roads disrupt this balance. The long, slender, glossy brown pine marten, the iconic gray wolf, and the noble spotted owl all need interior landscapes to survive.

Fragmenting landscapes also hurt migrating species. Birds, for example, help keep the insect population under control by eating, quite literally, tons of them every year. Spring is a bird's equivalent of an all you can eat buffet. The birds cull the number of insects that can spread disease, or harm our crops, while also helping to pollinate everything from flowers to fruit bearing trees. However, contrary to popular belief, birds don't migrate because they get cold; they migrate for better, easier to access food sources. If food is harder to get, or if birds find their traditional stomping grounds destroyed or irreparably changed, they simply stop coming. Habitat fragmentation creates the odd situation where birds stop migrating even as insect populations spiral out of control.

"Spiral out of control" is a good analogy to describe our continued reliance on cars and the surrounding car culture. While roads, in moderation, help humans more than they hurt the larger planet, the sheer volume of roads that we've built and continue to build is problematic. And we build so many roads because we drive so many cars. Converting to hybrid cars or to electric cars isn't going to address this issue. Congestion, the main reason why we are building more and more roads, is the end result of too many cars, and changing what we use to fuel those vehicles isn't going to address the storm water runoff issue, the ecological fragmentation issue, and so on. A beautifully evocative poster developed by the city of Muenster, Germany shows that busses can carry the same number of people that it would take seventy-two cars.[28] Neither the Toyota Prius, the Nissan Leaf, nor any of the other current crop of "green" automobiles addresses the fundamental problems that cars take up a lot of space. Bicycles require 1/28th the parking space of a car, and are 2/3 more fuel efficient than cars, even when you consider that people need to eat more when transporting themselves by bike.[29] Walking is free, and would help to curb our current health epidemic, which is caused, in part, by too much food and too little exercise.

In cars, we have a technology that's expensive both for consumers and the government to maintain, is socially exclusive—poor people, children, the elderly and the ill cannot drive—dangerous, and, perhaps most importantly, is not our only option for transportation. Yet we continue to throw more resources behind making cars better or "greener" despite the overwhelming evidence that when you take the full picture of cars—even hybrid and electric vehicles—into account, it doesn't make much sense. From the tremendous amount of energy it takes to make cars, to the amount of energy it takes to keep them moving, to the way roads fragment landscapes, and consume tremendous amount of natural resources, cars are destructive for our planet. When faced with a poisoned apple you don't set about trying to make the apple less poisonous, you go and get yourself a peach.

In June 2008, Cookie Monster, a decades old character from the television series Sesame Street, appeared on the *Colbert Report* to explain his new, defining message. Namely, that despite his affinity for his eponymous dessert, the truth was that cookies should not be an everyday treat, but rather they were "a sometimes food." The revamping of Cookie Monster's image began in 2006, when criticisms arose that a character who unabashedly celebrated gluttony and poor eating habits was not necessarily to be championed in an America where an increasing number of children are facing a plethora of diet related illnesses ranging from hypertension to Type II Diabetes to a resurgence of rickets. If only there was an automobile monster to act as a similar type of spokesperson.

Car based communities have higher rates of obesity and reduced rates of social cohesion. And they pollute. They pollute when they're manufactured. They pollute when we build roads to drive on them. They pollute by allowing us to live ever further from urban cores transforming natural systems into subdivisions named for the swathes of nature that they destroy. And they do this regardless of how they're fueled. The hybrid car cannot save us from this reality—at best it can only prolong the descent. The truth is, the individual passenger cars are a bit like Cookie Monster's cookies. They're a sometimes tool. They're handy in specific circumstances, and sometimes they're just a sheer pleasure to drive, but they should not be used as the day-to-day source of primary transport for the majority of our citizens, and we certainly should not be designing our communities around them or finding ways to maintain and extend their reach.

5. HOW CLEAN IS YOUR CANTEEN?

I never drink water; that is the stuff that rusts pipes.
—W.C. Fields

Water has no taste, no color, no odor; it cannot be defined, art relished while ever mysterious. Not necessary to life, but rather life itself. It fills us with a gratification that exceeds the delight of the senses.—Antoine de Saint-Exuprey

When the well is dry, we know the worth of water.
—Benjamin Franklin

Spread across the vast area of the Central Brazilian Plateau, the Kayapó or as they prefer to call themselves, Mebengokre or "men of the water place," are perhaps the best-known indigenous tribe located within the Brazilian Amazon. The rock star Sting has sat down to talk with them. They've inked distribution deals with The Body Shop, and their images—brilliantly colored head dresses, bodies painted with inky black stripes, red face paint, and women with long flowing locks save for a distinctive V-shape shaved into the front of their hair—have become (for good or for bad) synonymous with the indigenous people of the Amazon.

Most of us in the US have only a passing relationship with the environment within which we live. We know little more than the vague rhythms of the seasons and almost nothing about the animals and plants with which we share an ecosystem and depend upon for our survival. The Kayapó by contrast, who inhabit land on both sides of the 1,230 mile long Xingu River in the northeastern state of Para Brazil, have carved out a society and lifestyle that is wholly connected to and dependent upon the Amazonian forest and grasslands where they live. You could take a New Yorker and plop him or her down in Boston and, except for developing a strong affinity for the Red Sox and a tendency to drop the r's in words such as "park" or "car," that person and their way of being would remain basically unchanged. The same cannot be said of the Kayapó. Their communities are typically located along the Amazon's main navigable rivers, in part because it's far easier to navigate a boat to the nearest village then to trek through the forest, but even more so for ecological reasons. Dependent on subsistence agriculture as well as fishing and hunting, the largest rivers provide the largest concentrations of fish and larger mammals to hunt. Unlike the New Yorker turned Bostonian, moving or displacing the Kayapó erodes their identity. Uprooting the forest pollutes the rivers, scatters the animals and in short makes their way of life all but completely impossible.

At the 1992 United Nations Conference on Environment and Development, better known as the Earth Summit (held, ironically, in Rio de Janeiro, Brazil) then President George H.W. Bush famously declared that "the American Way of Life" was not negotiable. But what about the ways of the Kayapó people—is their way of life non-negotiable? The Kayapó have taken a look at our way of living and have decided that they don't want it—and yet their way of life is increasingly being threatened. The forest is being cut down for cattle ranching and soybean cultivation, while increasingly the scourge of the Western world—the disposable plastic bottle—has made its way to the Amazon and is beginning to litter clog and choke its rivers and streams. It is ironic then, that bottled water with names like "Ice Mountain" and "Poland Spring," designed to convey the image of pristine wilderness, are quickly polluting the once pristine Amazon. It's still more ironic that our push to eliminate plastic water bottles may be doing the Kayapó and other people around the world as much harm as good.

Because of environmental concerns, over the past several years, there has been an increasing push to get people to reduce their purchases of bottled water. In 2007, New York City launched the $700,000 "Get Your Fill" campaign, to cajole New Yorkers to give up their bottled water habit and to drink tap water instead. The campaign, run by New York City-based dcf advertising and featuring ads extolling the virtues of tap water with phrases such as "great on the rocks" and "zero calories," sent teams around the city, armed with empty blue plastic bottles, to encourage people to fill the bottles with tap water instead of buying spring water. The campaign was a result of focus groups that revealed that the city's kids and immigrants failed to realize that New York City tap water—sourced from a system of 19 reservoirs and 3 lakes in upstate New York—was safe to drink. The CityStore, the official store of the city of New York, also began hawking "Drink NYC Water" decanters and water glasses, alongside I Love New York T-Shirts, and New York City Subway bucket hats.

New York City was not alone in its zeal. That same year, San Francisco and Salt Lake City both banned city departments and agencies from purchasing bottled water. The motivation was less because bottled water often robs local aquifers, effectively mining the water and generating local water shortages, while also, at least in the case of the Fiji brand, helping to prop up military juntas, and more because of the effect bottled water has on the waste stream. Plastic water bottles are one of the fastest growing sources of municipal waste. Each year 29 billion plastic water bottles, the equivalent of 17 million barrels of crude oil, or enough to power several hundred thousand automobiles, are produced for use in the United States.[1] Four-fifths of this plastic ends up in some combination of landfills and the world's oceans, where it never biodegrades because the insects, bacteria and enzymes which break down paper and other natural materials haven't yet evolved to eat plastic.

So what does eat this stuff? Simply put, we do. The plastic from our water bottles joins a seemingly endless stream of plastic products—plastic pellets deliberately added to shower washes and toothpastes for their "exfoliating" factor; plastic litter swept from our streets into our sewers; and nurdles, which are tiny flakes of pre-production plastic that will eventually be melted to produce plastic goods—which ultimately wind their way from our drains, sewers and harbors into the ocean. Once in the ocean, much of it ends up in one of at least five swirling patches of plastic, each at least the size of the state of Texas. With biodegradation impossible—even at the size of a mere molecule, plastic is too tough for nature to properly tackle—the plastic simply degrades, with the combination of sun, salt water and air breaking it into smaller and smaller pieces. Consequently, in some parts of the ocean, plastic particles outnumber plankton 6-to-1. Mistaking the plastic for plankton, fish consume it; those fish get eaten by other fish, which eventually get eaten by us.

At each stage of consumption, this toxic soup of endocrine disruptors—chemicals linked to diabetes, infertility, hormone disruption and much more—and cancer causing chemicals get more and more concentrated. As Charles J. Moore, founder of the Long Beach, California Algalita Marine Research Foundation, and someone who has highlighted the risk surrounding plastic in our oceans, points out, "It's not the big trash on the beach. It's the fact that the whole biosphere is becoming mixed with these plastic particles. What are they doing to us? We're breathing them, the fish are eating them, they're in our hair, and they're in our skin."[2]

Confronted with the reality that plastic water bottles were bad for the environment, harmful to human health, and increasingly costly for municipalities, the bottled water backlash became entrenched. In 2010, the town of Concord, Massachusetts went so far as to ban bottled water completely. In its stead, arose the, preferably metal, water bottle. What was once the domain of hikers, cyclists, and other athletes became a mainstream symbol both of one's environmental awareness and of one's commitment to personal health through proper hydration. While use of durable water bottles would seem a step forward for the Kayapó, in reality it obscures the fact that the materials for the durable water bottles have to come from somewhere. And that somewhere, unfortunately for the Kayapó, is their home. Since the 1980's, the Kayapó Para region has been encroached on for aluminum mining and smelting; where the aluminum industry goes, large swathes of forest are cut down, and rivers and lakes, which locals depend upon for food and transport, turn red with arsenic, chromium, and mercury laden silt.

The early water bottles of choice were actually made of plastic, usually manufactured by Nalgene, a maker of reusable laboratory plastic before the company turned urban outfitter. In 2005, there were whispers that some Nalgene bottles could leech Bisphenol A (BPA), an endocrine disrupter that can mimic the body's own hormones, potentially causing thyroid problems and cancer. By 2008, the risks of Bisphenol A went nationwide, and millions of people chucked their hard-to-recycle water bottles (plastic bottles are not recycled by many municipalities). Some switched to Nalgene's BPA free plastic bottles, while others headed to the burgeoning stainless steel water bottle manufacturer Klean Kanteen. Meanwhile, others headed to companies such as Sigg, which manufacturers aluminum water bottles in a variety of decorative prints, making them the stylish choice for the design conscious, environmentally aware individual.

Yet, despite the fact that Sigg boasts of the recyclability of their aluminum water bottles—and to be clear, aluminum is completely recyclable—their bottles are made from 100 percent virgin aluminum. Consequently, each 150 gram, 1 liter Sigg bottle releases roughly .77pounds of carbon before it's even left the aluminum smelter, and that's not taking into account the energy that Sigg consumes in shaping, decorating, and shipping the bottles from their manufacturing plants in Switzerland. In fact, a 1999 MIT study showed that producing one ton of virgin aluminum generates approximately 10 times more carbon dioxide than the production of a ton of steel (recycled aluminum in contrast would only utilize 5 percent of the energy that virgin aluminum does).[3]

Even ignoring the carbon footprint, aluminum manufacturing is a particularly dirty business. When one first sets eyes upon an open pit mining operation—the kind favored by the aluminum industry—the sheer size of the endeavor astounds the senses. Large lumbering pieces of equipment with names like "The Excavator" shift massive chunks of earth in a manner previously only accomplished by glaciers, earthquakes and Greek gods. The degree to which open pit mining drastically changes the landscape is stunning in its audacity. Soil is removed, trees are upended and the terrain is artfully molded, albeit by a deranged landscape architect seeking to evoke a Mad Max-style dystopia.

The process of open pit mining is more or less what it sounds like—you simply grab a shovel and start digging until you find bauxite, the main mineral or ore used in aluminum manufacturing. Open pit mining is the preferred method for mining bauxite, because unlike say coal, which tends to (though not always) reside deep underground, bauxite lies relatively close to the surface, so digging is one of the easiest ways to access the material. The pit is vast because an aluminum mine continues to expand until it's exhausted its supply of bauxite, or until the piles of discarded dirt, rocks and debris that aren't bauxite becomes a burden.

The aluminum mining industry wants us to believe that it is as safe and clean as an extractive industry can be. A perusal of the International Aluminum Institute's Fourth Sustainable Bauxite Mining Report paints a downright rosy image of the industry, complete with pictures of mines turned, as if by magic, back into forest.[4] In fact, the aluminum mine manufacturer Alcoa won the United Nations Environmental Programme's (UNEP) Global 500 Roll of Honor for Environmental Achievement in 1990 for its reforestation of its bauxite mines in Western Australia. Unfortunately, Alcoa also has quite the corporate rap sheet, involving pollution and social destruction. In 2003, the company was found guilty of violating the Clean Air Act by releasing some 104,000 tons of emissions, including 40,000 tons of smog producing nitrogen dioxide and heavy metals, including lead, at its Rockdale Aluminum smelter near Austin, Texas.[5] In Canada, toxic run-off from Alcoa aluminum smelters is thought to cause extremely high rates of cancer among beluga whales in the St. Lawrence River.[6] And Alcoa is not the only company reaping such environmental havoc. In 2010, the Western Hungarian villages of Somlovasarhely, Kolontar, and Devecser were flooded by 6-foot high waves, which released more than 35-million cubic feet of sludge made up of arsenic, cadmium and lead from a nearby aluminum smelting owned by MAL Magyar Aluminum. The country's worst chemical disaster killed nine people, injured more than 100, poisoned farmland and contaminated Hungary's second longest river, the Danube, while also putting downstream neighbors Croatia, Serbia and Romania at risk.[7]

Smelting, or the process of extracting aluminum from its oxide alumina, isn't just toxic—it is also extremely energy intensive. The cheapest way to produce the vast quantities of electricity necessary for aluminum smelting is to build a hydro-electric damn and locate the smelter next to the dam. A fact that brings us back to the Kayapó, as the Para region of Northern Brazil that they call home is increasingly the seat of aluminum smelting. Within that region, Alcoa has razed a 3300 foot wide, 35 mile long swath of virgin Brazilian rainforest to haul bauxite ore mine to the coast. The Brazilian government's push to build the Belo Monte Damn—which would be the third largest damn in the world—is in large part motivated by a desire to power aluminum smelting mines in Northeastern Brazil.[8] Never mind that the damn will flood 150 square miles of agricultural land and forest, displace over 20,000 people, cause a permanent drought on the Xingu River's "Big Bend," directly affecting the Paquiçamba territory of the Juruna indigenous people, and spur deforestation of what was once flourishing rainforest. That the Amazon is often referred to as the lungs of the world and absorbs some 1.5 billion tons of carbon dioxide has not stopped Alcoa from beginning work on a mine that will destroy 10,500 acres of primary rainforest and suck 133,407 gallons of water per hour.[9]

To be clear, while water bottles alone are not causing this mess, they're contributing to the problem by adding one more item to the demand for aluminum. It's not just Sigg or aluminum water bottles that are to blame either. Most water bottle manufacturers have problematic sourcing. For example, stainless steel bottle retailer Klean Kanteen may boast about its wind powered webhost and its Forest Stewardship Council (FSC) certified in-store displays, but like Sigg, its water bottles contain no recycled material. This is a problem because stainless steel, like aluminum is extremely resource intensive. While aluminum is composed primarily of bauxite, stainless steel is an alloy composed mostly of iron, nickel, and chromium. Nickel mining occurs in the same manner as aluminum mining (open pits) and iron smelting is notoriously toxic. Similarly, Nalgene's new BPA Free water bottles (Everyday Nalgene) are still made from a difficult to recycle #7plastic. Most curbside recycling programs won't take them, and unlike aluminum, plastic is not 100 percent recyclable, as you always have to add new plastic to the old plastic. Consequently, Nalgene's bottles contribute to the same problems as disposable water bottles, albeit at a slower rate.

There is also the problem that durable water bottles haven't succeeded in doing the one thing that they was supposed to do—reduce our consumption of bottled water. Despite aggressive efforts on the parts of local governments and advocacy groups such as Food and Water Watch, and increasing sales of water bottles, Americans reduced their consumption of bottled water by a mere 1.1 percent , from 8.8 billion gallons of bottled water in 2007 to 8.7 billion gallons of bottle water consumed in 2008.[10] That number dipped still further in 2009, to 8.45 billion gallons, but by 2010 Americans were consuming just as much water as before— 8.75 gallons billion gallons—causing many to conclude that the dip in consumption was likely due as much to economic conditions as to a shifting in cultural currents regarding bottled water consumption.[11] It seems, then, that our use of water bottles is additive, not reductive. We are using water bottles in addition to, not instead of, bottled water.

To be fair it doesn't have to be this way. In 2001, for example, Americans threw out roughly 51 billion single use aluminum cans (more than 50 percent of the cans we used). If we just recycled those cans (and if companies would use recycled aluminum), durable water bottles could be a lot greener. But they aren't, and we should be more concerned with how things are as we are with how things could be.

It doesn't seem so long ago that water bottles—of any stripe—were the domain of athletes and outdoors people. Given that we spend 87 percent of our time indoors, within spitting distance of clean drinking water and this old fashioned thing called cups, why do most of us need water bottles? Instead of boldly declaring our greenness by purchasing a water bottle, isn't it greener to do what we did before we all strolled through town with bottled water in tow: drink from public drinking fountains, or out of glasses at home and at work, or simply, be thirsty for awhile until we can get to a water source? Could it be that the latter keeps us consuming, while the former does not?

6. THE GREENEST BUILDING

> *A man builds a house in England with the expectation of living in it and leaving it to his children; we shed our houses in America as easily as a snail does his shell.*
> —Harriet Beecher Stowe

> *His house was perfect, whether you liked food, or sleep, or work, or story-telling, or singing, or just sitting and thinking, best, or a pleasant mixture of them all.*—J.R.R. Tolkien

> *Our houses are such unwieldy property that we are often imprisoned rather than housed by them.*—Henry David Thoreau

> *Suburbia is where the developer bulldozes out the trees, and then names the streets after them.* —Bill Vaughn

Jay Shafer designs and builds small houses. Extremely small houses. Tumbleweed Tiny House Company, the home design and building company that he founded, only builds homes up to 837 square feet—roughly one third the size of the average home built in 2009.[1] Shafer's own home, an astonishing 89 square feet is, by his own admission, smaller than some people's closets. His decision to live in such a tiny space arose from concerns he had about "the impact a larger house would have on the environment, and because I do not want to maintain a lot of unused or unusable space. My houses have met all of my domestic needs without demanding much in return. The simple, slower lifestyle my homes have afforded is a luxury for which I am continually grateful."[2]

Shafer's tiny houses, which through careful planning and thoughtful design meet all of the comforts of modern living, remain the exception not the rule, as our present day culture, for the most part, admires and exalts the big. In 1950, the average sized single family home was 1000 square feet—just slightly larger than the largest of Jay Shaffer's houses.[3] By 1974, the size of the average new single family home had climbed to 1700 feet square feet.[4] Fast forward nearly a quarter century to 2007, and average housing size had ballooned to 2500 square feet, before drifting south in 2009, for the first since 1994, to 2400 feet.[5] (This downshift was likely motivated at least in part by the recession, as housing size declined during the recession of the 1990s as well.[6]) But even at 2400 square feet, the average American home today looms much larger than its counterparts of half century ago. And, if you were thinking that the reason for this growth in house size is due to increased population, think again; the average household in 1950 held 3.37 people, while in 2009, that number had decreased 24 percent to 2.57 people.[7] Houses have gotten larger even as family size has shrunk.

This growth in housing size has been buoyed, in part, by the rise in particularly large homes, what some sneeringly deride as "hummer houses," "McMansions," or "starter castles." For example, while in 2005 the average size for new houses was 2400 square feet, hidden within that average is the fact that 1 in 5 of those houses, or 20 percent, was larger than 3000 square foot. That's more than three times larger than the size of your average 1950s home. By the early 2000s, these houses, a broad expanse of four to ten thousand square feet—though some, including *New York Times* columnist Thomas Friedman's 11,400 square foot house in suburban Maryland home and developer Robert A.M. Stern's 11,870 square foot home in the Riverdale section of the Bronx are even larger—with vaulted ceilings soaring as high as fifteen feet in the air, had migrated to cities and suburbs around the country.[8] A 2007 study in the *Journal of Urban Design* found that in a survey of officials from 29 of the 50 largest US cities, two-thirds had reported the appearance of McMansions within their municipalities.[9] Once predominantly the domain of wealthy enclaves on the eastern most shores of Long Island, the ski slopes of Aspen, and the affluent suburbs of Connecticut, suddenly cities like Atlanta, Houston, and Phoenix had to contend with these spacious houses. Even in notoriously tiny housed New York City, the craze for ever bigger homes in the city's outer boroughs forced local council boards to create new zoning requirements that limited house size to a specific percentage of lot size.[10]

Given that house size has increased even as family size has declined, we can conclude that the reason our homes have gotten larger is not based on need. Whether it's due to overzealous developers or home buyers intent on impressing, however, the outcome is the same—environmental degradation. And, as with much that we do without considering the larger picture, our homes tend to be rough on the earth. While we often think of houses as relatively simply structures made of brick or wood, in fact, the modern home is comprised of many potentially hazardous materials. For example, Polyvinyl chloride (PVC) and its cousin Chlorinated Polyvinyl Chloride (CPVC) are routinely used to make everything from vinyl siding to plumbing pipes to the flooring underfoot. PVC is a vinyl chloride composed of chlorine, carbon, and hydrogen, to which a myriad of chemicals such as lead, cadmium and phthalates—a group of chemicals known as "plasticizers" used to make plastics like PVC more flexible and resilient—are added. The resultant product is one which is hazardous at every stage of its lifecycle: its production exposes workers and surrounding communities to chemicals that have been linked to cancer, endometriosis, neurological, immune system, liver and kidney damage, respiratory problems and birth defects.[11]

"Cancer Alley," the dubious title given to the once unsullied Mississippi River coastline stretching some eighty miles from

New Orleans to Baton Rouge, is now one of the most polluted areas of the United States due in no small part to the vinyl industry. In this part of the country, children go to school with respirators, the obituaries section is filled with the latest round of cancer fatalities and entire towns, viewed as too toxic, are literally bulldozed off of the map. Dioxin, a group of chemically-related compounds that are a byproduct of PVC production and incineration and have been labeled by the World Health Organization as persistent environmental pollutants that can cause reproductive and developmental problems, damage to the immune system and cancer, have been found in fish in the area's waters, as well as in pets and farm animals.[12] Dioxin is also a bioaccumulative, which means it accumulates in the fatty tissue of animals so when we eat those animals, it builds up in our systems too.[13] These chemicals don't remain locked in the vinyl either, but leak into the air, a process known as "off gassing," as well as into water supplies from landfills or into the atmosphere during incineration, harming the larger environment at every step of their existence.

It doesn't end with PVC. Until 2004, when the use of arsenic was disallowed for residential and general consumer construction, the pressure treated wood used to build backyard decks and other outdoor wood structures was bathed in arsenic based solutions that not only retarded the decay of the wood, but also exposed people to the risk of arsenic poisoning. Over time, the arsenic often migrates from the wood into the surrounding soil and can, according to the EPA, be dislodged from the wood surface upon contact with skin.[14] While the use of arsenic is now limited in home applications, it's still legal for commercial use.

Volatile Organic Compounds, or VOCs, are carbon compounds that can become airborne even at room temperature. These chemicals cover a wide number of compounds, some of which are harmless or even beneficial, as in the case of VOCs emitted by forests. However, the VOCs emitted in the home, including chemicals such as acetaldehyde, toluene, isocyanates, xylene, benzene, and formaldehyde, when inhaled, can cause a host of medical problems ranging from liver, kidney and nervous system damage to an increased risk of cancer.[15] Formaldehyde, for example, is known to cause cancer and yet it is used as a binder in composite wood and batt insulation. Toulene, a solvent commonly used in paint thinners, is associated with an increased risk of lung cancer, while xylene, which is used to make fiberglass based materials including insulation, is associated with an increased risk of non-Hodgkin's lymphoma. The smell that many of us associate with "newness" is one we should in fact associate with illness.

Further, the problem with the "greenness" of our homes does not begin and end with toxicity. Home building, it turns out, is also extremely energy and resource intensive. Making drywall, the material used to construct the interior walls in most homes, accounts for one percent of the total annual energy consumption in the US, emitting some 25 billion pounds of CO2 each year.[16] According to the US Green Building Council, buildings account for 38 percent of annual CO2 emissions—more than the transportation or industrial sectors—with the picture growing still bleaker when the manufacture and transport of building construction and demolition materials, as well as transportation associated with sprawl, are factored in.[17] In total, buildings account for 72 percent of electricity consumption, 39 percent of energy use, 40 percent of raw materials use and 14 percent of annual drinkable water consumption.

Considering that your typical building lasts between fifty and one-hundred years, finding a way to build less resource intensive buildings seems like the eco-friendly thing to do. Consequently, as realization of the heavy environmental impact of home building grew, so too did the concept of green building. As a practice, green building means increasing the efficiency of energy, water and materials use, with the goal of reducing the negative impacts of building on human health and the environment.[18]

Leading the way in modern green building design is the US

Green Building Council's LEED, or "Leadership in Energy and Environmental Design" certification program. Internationally recognized, the council provides third-party verification that a building or community is designed and built (or retrofitted) using strategies intended to improve performance in metrics ranging from energy savings, water efficiency, CO2 emissions reduction, improved indoor air quality, and good resource stewardship. There are a total of nine different LEED subjects—New Construction, Existing Buildings: Operations and Maintenance, Commercial Interiors, Core and Shell, Schools, Retail, Healthcare, Neighborhood Development, and Homes, split amongst five categories: Green Building Design and Construction, Green Interior Design and Construction, Green Building Operations and Maintenance, Green Neighborhood Development, and Green Home Design and Construction.[19] Under this system, buildings and structures are given a LEED rating, with the lowest level being "certified," increasing there from "silver" to "gold" to "platinum." Successfully reaching a given LEED certification requires a subject property to score specific point totals, which differ among building types. There are a number of potential points available for various green building practices, ranging from installing bike racks on site to properly sourcing materials, such as the iron ore in steel, from sustainably mined sources.

LEED is at least partly responsible for the increased use of alternative, potentially gentler on the earth materials such as bamboo flooring instead of wood, recycled denim insulation instead of fiberglass, and low VOC and milk (casein) based paints. The LEED standard has reached such widespread recognition that some municipalities require all new buildings be built to LEED standards even if they don't seek actual certification. Achieving LEED certification isn't just about building to a LEED standard, but also about paying the USGBC for verifying that the building was indeed built to said standards. Consequently, some buildings unwilling to pay for the actual certification may claim to be "built to LEED standards" even if they don't receive official certification. In total, there are now some 4,825 LEED certified buildings in the US, ranging from Los Angeles's Getty Center to a LEED certified floor in New York's iconic Empire State building.[20]

Even individual homes have gotten into the act. When first conceived in 2000, LEED was primarily focused on office buildings and other large structures. In 2008, the LEED for Homes program was established with a focus on the design and construction of high performance, multi-and-single family housing. There are now 10,161 LEED certified homes across the country.[21] These projects range from the ultra ambitious Playa, a 4,300 square foot home laboratory built in the car dependent community of Westchester, California, made by "deconstructing" an existing single-family home—i.e., taking it apart board by board, nail by nail. Usable building products are donated and recycled, diverting material from the landfill.[22]

According to the project's developers, "We're studying the sun, the winds and the neighborhood, and we're incorporating everything into the design and build of our new home. Plus we're greening it all—from solar roof panels to recycled content countertops in the cutting edge cook's kitchen."[23] On the more conventional side of the scale rests Philadelphia's 1,200 square foot LEED Platinum 100k houses which were designed for efficiency, environmental sustainability, and affordability for the first time home owner (The 100K references the target price of the structures).

Despite LEED's ubiquity, it is not the only sustainable building standard around. The Green Globes system, overseen in the United States by the Green Building Initiative, is a program designed to provide "practical and affordable" guidance in advancing the overall environmental performance and sustainability of green commercial buildings.[24] The certification, which relies heavily on a web based assessment application, applies to new construction as well as to existing buildings, with buildings that meet 35 percent of the protocols achieving certification.

A building standard that is more focused on homes is Passive House, which was first made popular in Germany and is officially certified by the Passive House Institute. The name refers to the way the buildings are primarily heated and cooled—passively. This means that the structures are well insulated and all but airtight, reducing the likelihood of energy loss through leaks and cracks. In the winter months, passive houses are heated primarily by solar energy— the homes are situated in such a way that, in conjunction with the heavy insulation and lack of normal air leaks, they can be heated almost exclusively by the sun, as well as from the body heat of the structure's inhabitants. Consequently, energy losses are minimized, while any additional heat can be provided by an extremely small energy source such as a pellet heater. In the summer months, heat gain is avoided through shading and window orientation, which also reduces the need for air conditioning. Given how tightly sealed the houses are, to avoid the suffocation of the structure's occupants—as well as the poor indoor air quality that often accompanies tightly sealed buildings—a small ventilator (similar to the HVAC systems in big buildings) provides a constant balance of fresh air. Although a relatively new design concept to the United States, several passive house structures already exist. For example, University of Louisiana architecture professor Corey Saft built a 1,200 square foot, three bedroom, two bath passive house in Lafayette, Louisiana that uses 90 percent less energy than a comparable conventional structure.

All of these different green standards, however, are not without their detractors. For example, LEED buildings rely heavily on energy projections to determine the future savings of buildings. However, once in actual use, buildings may differ substantially from the projections and often use far more energy in practice then they were predicted to. Despite this increased energy use, such a building would still maintain its LEED certification. In addition, even in the cases when buildings are properly designed and activity matches projections, energy backsliding may occur because of how the building is maintained and run, especially with larger buildings, where systems have to be run and maintained properly.

Another criticism of LEED, which by proxy extends to Green Globes, is that since both are additive points based systems—you get points for being more ecologically efficient than similar "non-green" buildings—there is little incentive for designers to consider utilizing even better systems. Thus, building designers can continue to do the same old thing, but if they do it more efficiently, they can slap a "green" label on it, in much the way car manufacturers trotted out hybrid engine SUVs. While the cars are more efficient, they are still a long way from what any thinking person would consider green. Buildings can earn points, for example, by including secure bicycle parking, but if the structure is located too far away for employees to cycle to work, what is the real environmental benefit?

In 2008, mechanical systems designer Henry Gifford wrote a paper arguing that in contrast to the US Green Building Council's claim that LEED certified buildings on average use 25 to 30 percent less energy than similar non-LEED buildings, in reality, most LEED buildings have shown an energy savings of only 15 percent, while roughly a quarter of LEED buildings actually use 29 percent more energy than most similar buildings in the dataset. Wrote Gifford:

> Going to so much trouble and expense to end up with buildings that use more energy than comparable buildings is not only a tragedy, it is also a fraud perpetuated on US consumers trying their best to achieve true environmental friendliness. Worse, by spending so many years without measuring anything, and then obscuring the truth when data is finally available, the USGBC has

> squandered the tremendous public good will that has accumulated behind the cause of environmentally friendly buildings.[25]

To date no one, not even the USGBC, has claimed that Gifford's technical findings were incorrect.

This sort of faux greenness doesn't just happen in office buildings. The Solaire, a New York City apartment building built in 2003 and LEED certified "Gold" in 2004, was billed as "America's first environmentally advanced residential tower." As part of that goal, the building was built with solar panels to generate at least some of the building's electrical energy. However, for solar panels to be effective they need sunlight, which is why we don't put solar panels in our basements. The presence of sunlight, however, is not enough. In photos of solar arrays, one of the most noticeable things is that the panels are generally tilted upwards towards the sun, the way a sunbather will sit in a tilted lawn chair to catch maximum rays. The degree of tilt in which a solar panel can catch the most amount of sunlight is known as the solar angle. A correct solar angle is critical because solar panels consume a tremendous amount of energy and resources in manufacture—their benefit lies in the fact that over time they will produce enough energy to offset that energy and resource drain. Poorly situating a solar panel severely limits its effectiveness.

In the case of The Solaire, the building was constructed with many of its solar panels laid vertically, that is flat against the building, where they would be viewable from the street thus announcing the building's greenness, instead of tilted at an ideal solar angle where they would actually generate enough energy to truly be green. Consequently, they produce only a fraction of the electricity than they would have if mounted at the correct solar angle. In addition, many of the panels aren't facing south (the direction with the most sun exposure) but rather southwest, or even northwest, which because they receive less sunlight, also renders them less effective. Another group of panels is positioned such that rooftop equipment throws shadows on at least one of the panels at all times, also rendering those panels less effective. In short, the Solaire manages to get the accoutrements necessary to move towards sustainability, but does so in such a way as to not actually be green.[26]

Similarly, many modern skyscrapers feature sleek exteriors made completely out of glass because they are aesthetically desirable, and are also far easier for architects to design. Unfortunately, when it comes to providing buildings with the insulation necessary to keep heat out, or in, glass is not a good option. Providing as much insulation as using a pair of 2 x 4's and a layer of cheap, pink fiberglass insulation, glass is far from the optimum choice when it comes to choosing the material for a building's outer envelope. And yet its use—even amongst LEED platinum buildings—is widespread. As journalist Alex Wilson of *Environmental Building News* writes,

> Some of the world's most prominent 'green' skyscrapers, including New York City's One Bryant Park (the LEED Platinum Bank of America skyscraper) and the New York Times Tower, wear the mantle of green with transparent façades. But there is a high environmental cost to all that glitter: increased energy consumption....In general, heavily glazed buildings consumes more energy than buildings with more moderate levels of glass. With a higher glazing fraction, solar heat gain as well as heat loss in cold weather are both greater. Glass does introduce daylighting, of course, and well-executed daylighting can reduce both electric lighting and mechanical cooling costs but the ideal percentage of glazing is far below that of many of today's prominent all-glass buildings.[27]

The continued use of products like glass in buildings that are called green but only are in comparison to our currently inefficient practices, only serves to perpetuate a system that continues to normalize our extremely wasteful modern construction methods by championing minute gains in efficiency. It is a system in which the National Realty and Development Corporation of Purchase, New York can call Windermere, its LEED certified planned community "green" despite the fact that it features 7,000 square foot, four story, single family homes with three car garages.[28] It is also a system in which former Vice President, Nobel Laureate, environmentalist-at large and star of the Academy Award Winning climate change focused film *An Inconvenient Truth* Al Gore can label his 10,000-square-foot historic Nashville home "green" because it runs only on renewable energy—including the use of *thirty-three* rooftop solar panels and *seven* geothermal wells.

Ultimately, the single biggest determinant of how many resources a building will consume is its size. In much the same way that bigger cars require more energy and resources both in creation and in use, so too do bigger houses. Assuming average housing occupancy, greener structures are smaller structures. Furthermore, as we will touch upon shortly, renewable energy sources only work in conjunction with drastically reducing the volume of our energy needs. Consuming an exorbitant amount of renewable resources does little to reduce our dependence on fossil fuels. This is a lesson that Vice President Gore seems to have missed. (Although Mr. Gore manages to hold on to at least one green credential—his Tennessee home was a retrofit and not a new construction.)

Another problem with green construction is that much of the attention and support goes to developers who are building new structures, based on the notion that yesterday's buildings solved yesterday's problems, while tomorrow's buildings will solve tomorrow's problems. And yet, as Carl Elefante eloquently argues in a 2007 article in *The Journal of the National Trust for Historic*

Preservation, the greenest building is the one that has already been built.[29] There are a few reasons for this. The first is related to embodied energy or the total energy used to make a product. As journalist Wayne Curtis writes in a 2008 *Preservation* article,

> If embodied energy is worked into the equation, even a new, energy-efficient office building doesn't actually start saving energy for about 40 years. And if it replaces an older building that was knocked down and hauled away, the break-even period stretches to some 65 years, since demolition and disposal consume significant amounts of energy.[30]

This is why Mike Jackson, chief architect with the Illinois Historic Preservation Agency, argues that there's limited benefit to knocking down a solidly built old structure to build a new "green" one in its place. The likelihood of constructing a new building today that will last sixty-five years is slim, as most builders build with the expectation that a house will only last fifty years. Every year we can efficiently maintain an existing structure reduces the environmental load associated with building a new structure. Further, more than two-thirds of the building stock that will exist in a generation from now has already been built. It makes far more sense to devote time and attention to renovating the current building stock in a manner that increases its environmental efficiency than it does to pour billions of dollars into new construction in a manner that may or may not be holistically green.

In addition, older buildings are often more sturdily constructed than modern buildings. According to a 2008 article in *The Atlantic*,

> ...modern suburban houses, even high-end McMansions, are cheaply built. Hollow doors and wallboard are less durable than solid-oak doors and lath-and-plaster

> walls. The plywood floors that lurk under wood veneers or carpeting tend to break up and warp as the glue that holds the wood together dries out; asphalt-shingle roofs typically need replacing after 10 years.[31]

By contrast, many older, inner-city neighborhoods consist of "sturdily built, turn-of-the-century row houses, tough enough to withstand being broken up into apartments, and requiring relatively little upkeep."[32] In many cases, as a society, we prefer to embrace technological solutions to our problems. Based on this, modifying existing structures speaks to us less than building entirely new structures. Thus, many of the latest "build it green" techniques seem to focus on high tech approaches, such as some passive house designs that use top of the line ventilation systems complete with CO2 censors. When we focus on these technically oriented solutions, we ignore much simpler, traditional methods of green building that not only tread lightly on the earth, but are more easily within the financial reach of your average aspiring home owner.

For example, "rammed earth" is an ancient building technique in which soil mixtures are pounded into a form, and as the mixture hardens, the forms are removed and the resulting free standing structure forms the shell of the house. The method is similar to building a sand castle, only instead of flipping the bucket to remove the sand, the bucket has removable sides which pull away. Once everything is packed tightly, the forms are removed and what's left is a solid stable wall. The process is repeated until the entire house is complete. This is the same method that was used to build parts of the Great Wall of China, some of which is still standing 2,000 years later. Beyond the inherent sustainability of the materials—the dirt is usually made from soil excavated on site—what makes rammed earth construction uniquely green is what also makes it stand out, namely that the thick walls, which usually run between 18 and 24 inches (61cm) and contain excellent thermal mass, which makes them great at holding temperatures. This leaves rammed earth houses cool in summer without the need for air conditioner or a fan, and warm in winter without the need for much heating. Paired with passive solar design techniques that take into account the sun's different positions throughout the year to passively heat or cool a home, rammed earth homes use one-third as much energy as a conventional home, saving on energy bills.[33] The thick walls of rammed earth homes are also extremely fire-resistant because there are no flammable components in the earth and the materials have been packed so tightly there's little chance of combustion. They are also termite proof because there is no wood, which also means there's no need for toxic chemicals to treat the surfaces.

Rammed earth isn't the only low-resource house building method around. Despite the bad rap that straw gets from the three little pigs, straw bale buildings are cheap, easy to build and extremely energy efficient. They resemble rammed earth houses with thick walls, wide window sills and rounded corners, but with additional insulation. They were first developed in the grasslands of Nebraska where there is plenty of straw and few trees. The structures are built by stacking bales of hay and then plastering the hay with plaster, stucco, or earth plaster. The resulting house is quiet (the thick walls provide natural sound resistance), warm, sustainable, and fire resistant—because the bales of hay are so tightly wound, they're exceedingly difficult to burn. While a typical wood framed structure can burn in as little as thirty minutes, a straw bale home will take two hours. They're also sturdy: many straw bale structures from the 1800's are still standing in the US and Europe today, and straw bale structures have withstood California earthquakes, as well as wind tests with sustained seventy-five mph gales. In addition, the United States burns or otherwise disposes of 200 million tons of "waste" straw annually, releasing carbon in the process. Using this easily renewable material (straw has a one year growth/harvest season) for house building would reduce our need to destroy slower growing forests; on average, a full acre of forest is used to build one 2,000 square foot single family home.

Another tree-free method, "cob building," dates back some 500 years and involves mixing clay-bearing earth with sand, straw and water to create a thick mud that can be hand sculpted into a house, which is then typically finished with stucco or plaster. Because of its free form, cob houses can (and do) look like just about anything the builder wants them to. Like other earth houses, the walls tend to be thick, resulting in a high thermal mass. Thus, cob houses are cool in summer and warm in winter, as well as being more energy efficient than frame houses. Additionally, because dirt is cheap, the houses are extremely cost-effective to build while also being fire and pest resistant.

Finally, if you've ever dreamed of living in a hobbit hole after one too many viewings of *The Lord of the Rings* movies, you're in luck—the building technique exists, and much like the hobbits' lifestyle, it's sustainable. "Underground" or "earth-sheltered" structures aren't just the function of J.R.R. Tolkien imagination, but rather have been around for centuries, taking on many different forms. Envelope houses consist of a central pit courtyard open to the sky with rooms tunneling off from the central courtyard. Slope houses are essentially a conventional home cut back into the side of a hill. All the windows and doors are on one side, while the back of the home—which lacks windows—is cut into the hill. The major benefit of underground construction is energy-efficiency. Because the earth stays at 50 degrees year round, earth houses maintain a consistent temperature, requiring next to nothing in the way of heating and cooling. Depending on location and size of structure, a few people and a greenhouse may provide all of the additional heating the dwelling requires, even in winter. Earth sheltered houses can cut energy use by as much as 85 percent.[34]

Despite the fact that all of the techniques we have just discussed are resolutely green, and have withstood the test of centuries, most builders won't use them, for a variety of reasons. Many insurers won't insure houses built from such materials, claiming lack of rigorous testing for flammability and structural soundness. It's also difficult to find lenders willing to extend financing, while most residential ordinances deem structures such as these illegal for similar reasons. That building codes would be so unyielding is unsurprising. After all, these codes are crafted, in part, by the developers least likely to benefit from these often-DIY structures. However, taken in tandem with a viewpoint that on the one hand acknowledges the need for buildings that are more energy efficient, use fewer chemicals and make more efficient use of natural resources, yet on the other hand seems to prioritize new buildings of questionable efficiency over retrofitting older already existing buildings—coupled with a populace who has a tendency of eroding gains in energy efficiency by simply demanding bigger houses—it becomes rapidly apparent that we have to move towards a more holistic definition of a green building than our current standards allow for.

Overall, what we can glean from looking at the larger green building landscape is that constructing more environmentally benign homes is *possible*. It is not, however, as straightforward as simply building a structure and leaving occupants to run with it. The LEED standards have shown that structures can look green on paper but fail miserably in execution. Therefore, we need to start asking deep questions about sustainability, moving away from an additive system that allows for significant wiggle room in labeling a building "green." In the case of large developments, we need third party verification systems that aren't based merely on projections, but that follow up and require buildings to perform up to or exceed expectations in practice.

We also need to educate consumers that an eight thousand square foot house is simply not green, and that placing such a building in the middle of nowhere, thus forcing occupants to drive long distances, is not green either, regardless of how many sustainably harvested wood frames, or formaldehyde free kitchen cabinets were used in its construction. Ultimately, we need to shift expectations as to what a building, and in the case of the average American, what a home, should look like. The suburban tract housing where every home on a block is near identical is a recent development, as is the idea that we should have homes in which many of the rooms are not used on a regular basis. A culture groomed on *Lifestyles of the Rich and Famous* and *MTV Cribs*, we have become far too accustomed to the idea of overbuilding, of homes echoing with rooms empty most of the time except for the stuff we have purchased to fill them.

It would be nice if we could shift the cultural pendulum to view this kind of excess as what it truly is—wasted space that requires energy to heat and cool, and nothing more. As Sarah Susanka, architect, and author of *The Not So Big House*, points out:

> So many houses, so big with so little soul. Our suburbs are filled with houses that are bigger than ever. But are bigger houses really better? Are the dreams that build them bigger or it simply that there seems to be no alternative?...a house is more than square footage and the number of beds and baths. In one of the wealthiest societies ever, many people are deeply dissatisfied with their most expensive purchase.

We have to demand better—for ourselves and for the environment.

PART II—FUELING THE FUTURE

7.THE CLEAN COAL MYTH

Here in the United States, we have between 250 and 300 years of a coal supply. That is more than the amount of recoverable oil contained in the entire world.—Tim Holden

I think of doing a series as very hard work. But then I've talked to coal miners, and that's really hard work.—William Shatner

In 2008, the American Coalition for Clean Coal Electricity, a coal industry front group, launched a series of television commercials intent on transforming coal's image from one that has never been associated with the word "clean," to one that was at the very least a greener shade of brown. This was no mean feat for a substance famous for giving industrial-era London it's gritty, grimy reputation. And who can forget the coal smudged face of Dick Van Dyke as the chimney sweep Burt in *Mary Poppins*? Affable chap as he was, not many would call him clean. And yet, "we can" intoned one commercial's announcer over a soundtrack of rising music calculated to puff the chest of even the most reluctant patriot "be energy independent. We can continue to use our most abundant fuel cleanly and responsibly. We can. We will. Clean Coal, America's Power."[1] Another commercial in the series sought to "educate" while also pandering to our jingoistic side. Over images of early airplanes spliced with that of stealth fighters, early room sized computers, juxtaposed against today's far smaller consoles the announcer declared, "Throughout history new ideas have often met with skepticism. But technology born from American ingenuity can achieve amazing things... we're committed to a future in which our most abundant fuel, coal, generates our electricity with even lower emissions."

If that doesn't just pull at your patriotic heart strings, you might as well move to Canada.

If it does pull at your patriotic heart strings, you can try moving to the eastern Pennsylvania town of Centralia. "Try" is the operative word because in 1992, when the Commonwealth of Pennsylvania reclaimed the borough and condemned all of its buildings, Centralia ceased to exist. The United States Postal Service revoked its zip code in 2002, and as of 2010, what was once a town of some 20,000 people is now home to a mere dozen.[2] In what used to be Centralia, positioned amidst pipes spewing upwards the noxious gas from below, trees bleached white from the heat and gasses, and earth so hot that not only does it smoke like something out of a horror film but it also lights a match upon contact without striking, is a sign cautioning: "Warning-Danger: Underground Mine Fire. Walking or Driving in this area could result in serious injury or death. Dangerous gasses are present. Ground is prone to sudden collapse."[3] What caused Centralia to cease to exist? In a word—coal.

Centralia's half century decline began in 1962 when local firemen set the community's dump, which was located in an abandoned strip mine pit, on fire, as they had done countless times in the past to reduce the escaping odors. They then extinguished the fire. Or so they believed. Instead, the fire spread through a hole in the rock pit into the town's underground network of abandoned coal mines. Below ground it grew in intensity—though not in national recognition—until 1981, when a 12-year old boy fell into a 45-foot sinkhole that suddenly appeared beneath his feet. The boy survived—his cousin managed to fish him out from the mouth of the hole before he could plummet to his death—but this incident brought the town's plight to the attention of the nation.[4] By 1984, Congress had allocated some $42 million dollars for the relocation of the residents of Centralia.

The kind of fire that literally extinguished the town of Centralia is known as a coal seam fire. Specifically it's what happens when an underground coal deposit catches fire. Not only is it all but inextinguishable, it's also sadly common. China, a nation that depends on coal for roughly 75 percent of the energy it uses to drive its economic engine, is home to some of the worst coal fires in the world. These fires, spread out in a thick belt across the continent, consume between 10 to 200 million metric tons (more precise numbers are impossible to pin down) of coal per year, or between .5 percent and 10 percent of China's total annual coal production, according to information released by the United States Geological Survey in September 2009.[5] In fact, one of China's largest coal seam fires, at the Terak mine in Xinjiang, a province in northwestern China, consumed as much as 12.5 million tons of coal and spewed out more than 70,000 tons of toxic gasses from the time it first ignited in the 1950's, until 2007, when Chinese authorities claimed it was extinguished.[6]

One would be hard pressed to call the heady mix of sulfur dioxide, nitrogen oxide, carbon dioxide, mercury, arsenic, fluorine and selenium released during these fires "green."[7] What the coal industry is basing its claims of "clean coal" on is a still unproven technology: carbon sequestration and storage, also known as carbon capture and storage. It is a practice that the US Department of Energy calls "one of the most promising ways for reducing the buildup of greenhouse gases in the atmosphere."[8] The principal is simple: If the problem with burning coal is carbon emissions, the solution then lies in eliminating those emissions. Carbon sequestration works by scrubbing the carbon from the atmosphere as coal is burnt, thus "capturing" the escaping carbon. That carbon is ejected into and stored in underground rock formations, in deep ocean masses, or in the form of mineral carbonates—safely out of the way of the upper atmosphere. The coal effectively stripped of its carbon emissions is now, the thinking goes, clean.

It is clean, if you ignore the fact that storing carbon in the deep ocean may increase ocean acidification, a problem that already occurs due to the overabundance of carbon in the atmosphere. Ocean acidification is linked to the mass extinction of marine species, including species that humans depend upon for their survival.[9] Carbon sequestered coal is clean if you ignore the reality that while we know that we can store carbon in rock formations, we don't know with certainty how long the carbon will remain embedded in our store houses, or if the carbon will eventually leak back into the atmosphere. Clean coal is clean if you don't take into account that the process of carbon capture and sequestration is so energy intensive that we would have to burn 10 to 40 percent more coal to sequester the carbon.[10] Finally, it is clean if you ignore the full lifecycle of coal production and focus only on one tiny aspect of its environmental footprint—its use. Yet the full production of coal is a dirty business, regardless of how we handle the emissions.

Take the aforementioned seam fire in Centralia. While human error was to cause of the fire, even if we could remove human activity from the equation, seam fires will continue to occur, as coal beds can be ignited by a multitude of natural events, including wildfires, lightning, and spontaneous combustion. These uncontrolled coal fires will continue to occur in the United States and in all coal-bearing parts of the world, spewing the very carbon into the atmosphere that "clean" coal advocates claim to be able to control. The more we dig and the more we expose coal seams, the more likely fires such as these are to occur.

Similarly, the issue with coal power plants does not begin and end with carbon emissions, as the residents who live along East Tennessee's Emory River could tell you. Early into the witching hour on December 22, 2008, just three days before Christmas, a dam at Tennessee's Kingston Fossil Plant, a coal burning electrical power plant, broke the dusky late night silence with a thunderous clap.[11] Residents would later say that they thought they were hearing two trains collide.[12] However, colliding trains would have caused less damage, as on that December night, the Kingston dam, a five-foot high earthen structure holding back an 84-acre pond filled with billions of gallons of coal ash slurry rising 65 feet into the air, failed spectacularly, unleashing half a century's worth—some one billion gallons—of wet coal ash onto the surrounding community. Homes were ripped from their foundation in the ensuing ash wave, and three hundred acres of land was buried six foot deep with wet gray sludge. The nearby Emory and Clinch Rivers were flooded with the toxic sludge and its endemic mix of arsenic, selenium, lead and radioactive materials.[13]

Coal ash is the gray powdery dust left over after burning coal. It's what remains after burning charcoal for a barbecue, and its cousin is what lingers in a wood stove after burning wood. It is also toxic, containing a mishmash of dioxins (which have been liked to linked to birth defects, spontaneous abortions and cancer), heavy metals such as lead (which causes developmental delays in children, insomnia, anemia and delayed growth), and mercury (which damages the central nervous system and is particularly dangerous to pregnant women and their unborn children). Coal-fired power plants are the single largest source of mercury pollution, accounting for over 50 percent of all mercury emissions.[14] In 2007, the EPA found that unlined coal ash waste ponds posed a cancer risk 900 times above "acceptable" levels.[15] Needless to say, this isn't particularly what one wants to wake up to three days before Christmas—least of all in a region where locals depend upon the river for the tourism dollars brought in by swimming, kayaking and fishing.

The Tennessee Valley Authority dealt with the issue by dredging the coal ash out of the river and shipping it by train to a landfill in Uniontown, Alabama. Uniontown is located in Perry County, one of the poorest counties in one of the poorest states in the nation. Nationally, according to 2008 Census Bureau data, the median household income is $52,029 and 13.2 percent of Americans (18.2 percent of children) live below the poverty line. In Perry County, however, the median household income stands at $26, 513, or roughly half the national average, while a third (31.7 percent) of residents and almost half of the children under the age of 18 (45.2 percent) live below the poverty line.[16] The county is also almost 70 percent African American. Perry County is so economically downtrodden that it made a certain kind of perverse sense that when it came time to find someplace to dump all of the coal ash from the Kingston Fossil Plant spill, the powers that be, including Perry County's own local government—many of whom have since been ousted—decided that Uniontown would benefit economically from being the recipient of all that ash. In fact, Perry's County Commissioner Albert Turner, Jr., a swaggering man whose voice booms with bravado explicitly stated "the concerns that I have is that I've got these many people unemployed in my county and that now I've found the opportunity to help ease that unemployment."[17] In 2009, Turner testified before Congress that the coal ash had reinvigorated Perry County's economy and that, "Now that Perry County is poised to join the ranks of the haves, those naysayers shout environmental racism. It would be economic racism if EPA or TVA stopped the flow of cash for ash."[18]

Never mind that since the TVA began moving coal ash into Uniontown in July of 2009 the unemployment rate in Perry County has actually *increased* slightly from 19.3 percent to 19.6 percent, according to Department of Labor statistics.[19] And this ignores the startling reality that everyone in Uniontown and the surrounding area now has to bear the health repercussions of living downwind from a toxic dump regardless of whether or not they gained a job from the dump. Residents now have the pleasure of not only breathing in the acrid smell of the fly ash, but of also having it blown around their neighborhood, as fly ash drifts from the dump and coats the surrounding community's cars and homes. As a result, people have to keep their windows firmly closed even in summer to keep the ash and fumes out, while activists plead for the coal ash's removal and implore the EPA not to make Perry County the "Ash Hole of Alabama."[20]

Despite the situation near the Emory River (and in Perry County), it's not just combustion that's a problem with coal. Anyone who has had the misfortune of driving through a coal mining town—especially one ravaged by the practice known as mountaintop removal mining—would be hard pressed to find anything "green" or "clean" about the practice. If you're unfamiliar with mountaintop coal removal, it is a four step process in rapid environmental destruction with a geographic range from Ohio to Virginia, though it is most heavily concentrated in West Virginia and Eastern Kentucky. It is perhaps as destructive an industry practice could be without simply engaging in destruction for the sake of destruction. As one hedge fund analyst who covers the coal market informed me in earnest, "Mountain top coal removal doesn't have many more years left in it. We're running out of suitable mountains to blow up." What precisely does the practice entail?

> **Step 1: Clear-cut the forest**. At this stage trees are chopped down, topsoil is scraped away and all plant life is destroyed along with any wildlife that can't scurry out of the way of the bulldozers. Explosives—approximately 2,500 tons of ammonium nitrate and fuel oil—are used every day, equivalent to the power of a Hiroshima bomb exploding every week. These explosives are then employed to blast up to 800 vertical feet of mountaintop.[21] To put this in perspective, if Mount Everest, which towers at roughly 29,000 feet, were to lose 800 feet of its mountaintop, it would no longer be the world's tallest mountain.

Step 2: Fill in the Valleys. Vast power shovels dig up any remaining soil while trucks haul away the material or push it into adjacent valleys.

Step 3: Harvest Coal. A dragline excavator, essentially a massive bucket suspended from a boom, exposes the coal while enormous machines weighing up to 8 million pounds with a base as big as a gymnasium and towers as tall as a 20-story building tear into the mountain to strip mine the coal. The heavy use of machinery replaces the need for workers—a small crew working day and night can decimate a mountain in less than a year, making short work of what took millennia to develop.

Step 4: Fill the Valley. Officially in this stage, coal companies are supposed to drag the rocks and other unwanted material (often called overburden) away from the site. In practice, mountain top removal's other name, "mountain-top removal and valley fill" comes from the tendency for coal companies to take all of the material they stripped off of the mountain top and dump it into the nearest valley—often blocking streams in the process. These valley fills can be more than a mile long, over a thousand feet wide and contain as much waste and debris as to fill almost 78,000 Olympic-sized swimming pools.

In total this practice—which makes up almost 50 percent of coal production in central Appalachia—allows for the rapid mining of coal while in the process destroying forests, polluting streams, fracturing habitats, and basically making a mess of one of the most hauntingly beautiful places in the continental United States. According to the Natural Resources Defense Council, more than 500 mountaintops have already been destroyed, while well over two thousand miles of Appalachian headwaters have been buried or polluted by mountaintop removal.[22] Only one mountain, Coal River Mountain, remains intact within the Coal River Watershed, and a battle is now being waged for its survival.

In its wake, mountaintop mining has left behind polluted drinking water, reduced jobs (mountain top coal removal employs far fewer people than traditional mining) and threatens the health and safety of all who make the region their home. Residents who live near such coal mines and drink from well water supplies have brain cancer rates several times the national average.[23]

Taken in total, it's clear that regardless of what coal industry lobbyists, government officials and even some scientists say, coal can never be "clean." It's certainly not green, and it is not something that anyone clamoring for a more sustainable future should throw their weight behind.

8. THE BIOFUEL REVOLUTION

> *Because we are now running out of gas and oil, we must prepare quickly for a third change, to strict conservation and to the use of coal and permanent renewable energy sources, like solar power.*—Jimmy Carter

> *We could have saved the Earth but we were too damned cheap.*—Kurt Vonnegut, Jr.

It's a unique twist of irony that while our civilization was built upon the carcasses of long dead organisms, in the form of fossil fuels, we now turn to the remains of recently living organisms, in the form of biomass, for our continued survival.

Contrary to popular belief, fossil fuels are not the remains of dead dinosaurs. Most in fact are the decomposed remains of dead plants and animals that walked, crawled, oozed, and otherwise inhabited the earth some hundred million years before T-Rex first roared.[1] Burning oil, coal and other fossil fuels pumps this ancient, previously sequestered carbon back into an atmosphere that has been functioning smoothly for quite some time without it. The introduction of this carbon fundamentally shifts the balance in our atmosphere, resulting in climate change.

Biomass is a renewable energy source derived from organic material, including garbage, wood, landfill gasses and alcohol fuels. What separates biomass from fossil fuels is the age of the carbon these products contain. Unlike fossil fuels, biomass is based on recent organisms that are already part of the carbon cycle. When biomass fuels are burned, additional carbon is not added to the atmosphere; instead, these fuels are simply returning the carbon that they had removed during their brief lifecycles—a concept known as carbon zero or net zero. When one considers the low-to-no carbon load of biomass, along with the fact that biomass generates energy in a manner that fits easily within existing energy infrastructures, it becomes clear why large industries—including the major oil companies—are increasingly throwing their support behind it.

In the United States, much of that support is being leant to one form of biomass in particular, which begins with corn. There is an ominous sort of beauty that comes from staring at a field planted with corn, row after row of tall emerald green stalks topped with feathery, golden fronds that ribbon across the landscape, suggesting living, healthy things, while also hinting at hidden things. It's fitting that cornfields, while are often used to represent the epitome of health, are also the setting for corn mazes, crop circles, and the horror film *The Children of the Corn*. Corn seems to conceal as much as it reveals. In the summer months, you can't travel very far outside of an American city without finding a field of corn, and even in a city as violently urbanized as New York, it's possible to find a stalk or two.

Yet, despite its presence in everything from tacos to Mountain Dew, no one is quite sure of the genetic route that corn traversed to transform itself from a weedy grass into the top heavy cob that would one day form a crucial piece of the global food web. What we do know is that by the time the first European conquerors set foot in the Americas, corn in its modern incarnation was already here and already a staple food poised to further cement its central role in human society. In the lower parts of North America and in Central America, corn was soaked in limewater to release vital nutrients, a process known as nixtamalization, and then ground and molded into flat breads or wrapped into tamales. Further north, in what is now the northeastern United States, corn was consumed not as tortillas but rather as puddings, mashes and soups. There's a reason why corn was so ubiquitous in North America—when paired with beans, it provided all of the protein necessary to sustain human life. Further, when corn grown together with climbing beans and squashes—a technique known as companion planting—in addition to being nutritious and delicious, formed a symbiotic relationship which simplified its cultivation.

Given its versatility, it makes sense that corn has expanded its zone well beyond the Americas. These days, it seems as though everyone grows at least some corn. For the year 2011-2012, some 866.2 million metric tons of corn was grown worldwide.[2] And yet, oddly, despite estimates which say roughly one fourth of the global population depends directly on corn for sustenance, very little of what is grown—roughly 20 percent—is consumed directly as food. Instead, much of it is used as animal feed, while an increasing amount of corn, by some estimates as much as 40 percent of the total US crop, is used to make a biomass, in the form of a biofuel known as ethanol.

Ethanol is a form of alcohol specifically modified for use as fuel, most commonly used for transportation. Formed from the sugars of grains, it can be made from sugarcane, sugar beets, barley, wheat, rice and potatoes, but in the US, due to its abundance, it is made almost exclusively from corn. (In Brazil, where sugarcane grows easily, sugarcane-based ethanol reigns supreme as a cheaper, cleaner alternative to conventional gasoline.[3]) In the United States, ethanol is blended into gasoline at concentrations between 5 and 10 percent, and as high as 15 percent in the summer months. If you've filled up your gas tank recently, particularly in the summer, you have undoubtedly seen signs at the pump noting that the fuel contains ethanol, allowing for a cleaner blend and improved air quality. What those signs on the pump won't tell you, however, is that ethanol contains less energy than gasoline, so you're also getting less oomph for the gallon.

However, proponents of ethanol, such as the agricultural giant Archer Daniels Midland and the ethanol trade industry group Renewable Fuels Association are quick to argue that in addition to ethanol's carbon neutral status, it is also far less toxic than fossil fuels, noting its heavy use in summer fuel blends to keep air pollution down during the time of year when heavy, muggy air is most likely to keep pollutants at breathing level. Says Jim Nussle, president of Growth Energy, an organization that represents the producers and supporters of ethanol, "If we truly want to reduce our dependence on foreign oil, create good-paying U.S. jobs and improve our environment, we need to ensure that our entire vehicle fleet is ready to use clean, renewable fuels like ethanol."[4] In many ways, Nussle is correct. After all, while we wonder how long we can continue to tap limited petroleum supplies in the face of increasing global consumption, ethanol is based on a renewable resource, as we can plant corn this year and next year and the year after that, ad infinitum. And unlike oil, which is only found in concentrated deposits that are all too often located within some of the most unstable and despotic regions of the world, corn can be grown locally. The local orientation of ethanol has another benefit—since plants are grown locally we can process biofuels locally as well. The rise of ethanol could eliminate the need for continent spanning pipelines and oil tankers which do unsavory things such as leaking toxic oil supplies into environmentally sensitive regions.

Unfortunately, ethanol loses some of its glossy sheen when you take a deeper look. According to Mark Jacobson, a Stanford University civil and environmental engineering professor, when it comes to smog and air pollution, ethanol is actually no better than gasoline, and may in fact fare slightly worse in urban areas where smog is already a problem, such as Los Angeles and the northeastern US, because it raises ozone levels more than gasoline does.[5] Though the science as to why is complex, at least part of the rise in ozone levels is related to the fact that burning ethanol produces more hydrocarbons, and ozone, a key component of smog, is the result of hydrocarbons, nitrogen oxide and sunlight. Sunlight is why smog is often worse in the summer and in hotter climates.[6] The irony, of course, is that urban areas are the very places, due to population density, that need a cleaner burning fuel.

In addition, it also takes a significant amount of energy to transform corn into the corn-based ethanol favored by the United States (over 90 percent of the ethanol made in the United States is corn-based).[7] According to the Department of Agriculture, for every unit of energy (typically fossil fuel based energy) used to make corn-based ethanol, the process generates 1.34 units of energy.[8] In other words, for every 100 units of energy we put into generating corn-based ethanol, we have 134 units of energy to show for our efforts, for a total increase of a mere 34 units of energy, or a 34 percent increase. If we were talking about stock portfolios, this would be a great return on investment, but since we're talking about energy, this is lousy. As a point of comparison, the world's most efficient form of transportation—a bicycle—is three times more energy efficient than the activity that it replaces (walking); substituting cycling for walking yields a net efficiency gain of some 300 percent.

In the case of corn-based ethanol, many critics argue that the calculations used to measure the 34 percent rate of return are inaccurate, and that the actual return is far worse, possibly even negative. A 2005 study by David Pimentel, a professor of Ecology and Agriculture at Cornell University, and Tad W. Patzek, a professor of Civil and Environmental Engineering at the University of California at Berkley, argued that the Department of Agriculture assessments rest on extremely positive underlying assumptions and that, in fact, in terms of energy output compared with energy input, corn-based ethanol consumes 29 percent more fossil energy than the fuel it produces.[9] This suggests that corn-based ethanol may result in a net energy loss, not an energy gain.

The energy picture for the sugarcane-based ethanol favored by Brazil is somewhat better. In contrast to corn-based ethanol's 20 to 30 percent—at best—rate of return, sugarcane-based ethanol has a rate of return of roughly 830 percent.[10] This rosy number, however, rests on some questionable assumptions, the most crucial of which is that the sugarcane is grown on already denuded tropical land. However, if we begin chopping down tropical rainforests (sugarcane can only be grown in tropical climates) to meet an increasing demand for sugarcane-based ethanol, those forests would release a tremendous amount of carbon emissions, eliminating any potential climate benefit. As it currently stands, according to the Food and Agricultural Organization of the United Nations, between 25 and 30 percent of annual global greenhouse gas emissions, or roughly 1.6 billion tons of greenhouse gasses, come not from burning oil or from burning coal, but rather from deforestation.[11] It turns out that tropical forests like the Brazilian Amazon, though traditionally thought of as carbon sinks, or locations that absorb carbon, if not properly maintained, become tremendous sources of CO2 emissions. This was illustrated by the Amazon drought of 2010, which spread across an area roughly seven times larger than the state of California and caused trees to die off so rapidly it not only inhibited the forest's ability to absorb carbon dioxide, but also released some 8 billion metric tons of carbon emissions into the atmosphere—2.6 billion more metric tons than the United States emitted total in 2009.[12] This was a level high enough to cancel out the carbon absorbed by the forests over the preceding decade, and, cautions Simon Lewis, the drought study's lead author and an ecologist at the University of Leeds, "If events like this happen more often, the Amazon rain forest would reach a point where it shifts from being a valuable carbon sink slowing climate change to a major source of greenhouse gases that could speed it up."[13]

Currently, in Brazil at least, sugarcane intended for ethanol is grown on land that has already been deforested. Yet increasing demand for ethanol, pushed in part by well-intentioned though often wrongheaded legislation, suggests that using forest land to grow sugarcane is likely only a question of time and demand. We need only look at palm oil production in Southeast Asia to see the problem.

Palm oil is a key ingredient in palm-based biodiesel, as well as in soaps and food products. In much the same way that we grow corn in large fields of monoculture, palm is grown in large swooping monoculture plantations, after first cutting down, burning and otherwise destroying the original peat swamp forest. Peatlands, better known as swamps or bogs, harbor substantial amounts of partially decayed vegetation, and are unique ecosystems which, in addition to playing host to a broad range of species (including the threatened orangutan), and maintaining fresh water supplies, are also true and vital carbon sinks. Although they only cover around three percent of the earth, they accumulate more carbon than tropical rainforests, storing as much as 500 billion metric tons of carbon or twice as much as is integrated into all the trees in all of the world's forests.[14]

A 2010 study looking at palm oil plantations in Malaysia, Borneo and Sumatra found that roughly 6 percent of the total territory had been deforested, leading to rapid biodiversity loss equivalent to the extinction of some 46 species and the release of some 140 million metric tons of carbon.[15] With the Indonesian government pledging to double palm oil production by 2020, this so-called "green" biofuel is poised to rapidly destroy large swathes of the regions' peat swamp forests, releasing tons of carbon dioxide and destroying a number of biologically diverse species in the process, while also illustrating one of the key problems associated with biofuels—they need to be grown. As the geneticist turned environmental activist David Suzuki points out "We use a lot of fossil fuels. Switching to bio fuels would not reduce the demand for fuel, just change the way we get it. And that would require a lot of land. In fact, substituting just 10 per cent of fossil fuels to biofuels for all our vehicles would require about 40 per cent of the entire cropland in Europe and North America."[16]

Ethanol production in particular depends upon the very kind of fossil fuel intensive, artificial pesticide and fertilizer dependent agricultural practices that we already know are ecologically problematic. Corn in particular is notorious for being a water and nitrogen hog. There's a reason why many Native Americans used intercropping or the practice of growing several different crops in the same space—because it worked ecologically. They grew corn with beans because beans fix nitrogen in the soil for the corn. Without this practice, corn rapidly sucks most of the nitrogen out of the soil, leaving it unfit to grow more corn, as well as any other crops.

And yet, most farms these days do not practice intercropping because the practice has one major drawback for the modern farm, namely that crops have to be harvested by hand, a process that leads to crops of different shapes and sizes. Most modern farm machinery these days is geared towards harvesting crops of nearly identical sizes, hence the heavy reliance on hybrid and genetically modified species, which can provide fairly consistent size and shape from generation to generation. Variety may be the slice of life, but it is the bane of farm machinery. Yet for ethanol to be commercially viable, it is necessary to grow and cheaply harvest vast acres of corn. To do that, you have to plant a field of nearly identical crops. In other words, you need to use monoculture. Harvesting by hand would raise the cost of ethanol to a point where it's no longer an economically viable fuel substitute. It's hard to imagine cars, for example, ever becoming popular, or four thousand square foot mansions seeming reasonable if the cost of fueling and heating them hadn't been so cheap. Alternative fuels only work as a direct substitute when they are both ecologically efficient and relatively cheap.

In order to plant corn in a way that is machine harvestable and meets our very narrow needs for cheap energy, copious quantities of artificial fertilizers must be used. Not only do we grind through a tremendous amount of fossil fuels to manufacture these fertilizers—fertilizer production accounts for 2 to 3 percent of natural gas consumption in the US, and about 5 percent worldwide—we also poison freshwater supplies in the process.[17] In a 2006 to 2008 sampling of Iowa wells, roughly half of the water samples contained detectable nitrate and ammonia levels.[18] Nitrates in drinking water inhibit the body's uptake of oxygen, and when water with nitrates is used to make baby formula, the result can be blue-baby syndrome, a potentially fatal respiratory and digestive condition which is caused when the nitrates in the water react with the oxygen carrying hemoglobin in the blood, forming high amounts of methemoglobin, which can deprive infant tissues of oxygen.[19] Water contaminated with nitrates has also been linked to reproductive problems, kidney disorders, and bladder and ovarian cancers.[20] Further, nitrogen oxides which are released when fertilizer is applied to soil not only act as a greenhouse gas, but also contribute to smog formation and react with water in the atmosphere, forming acid rain.

Yet, even with the application of artificial pesticides and fertilizers, you cannot continually plant corn on the same plot of land, as the soil eventually becomes devoid of nutrients. To try and get around this problem, many farmers, instead of planting a full field of corn every year, are planting fields of soy in alternating years. Since soy is a legume, or bean, it pulls nitrogen from the air and fixes or binds the nitrogen in the soil, augmenting the artificial nitrogen-fertilizers needed to grow corn. While soy cannot be turned into ethanol, it can be turned into biodiesel, an oil type fuel which can power cars and even heat homes. However, soy-based biodiesel is not a particularly efficient energy source. The Pimentel study found that soybean plants require 27 percent more energy than the fuel they produced.[21]

Perhaps most damaging on a human level, as we consume more and more ethanol, we hurt many of the same people already suffering in the wake of climate change by sending food prices soaring, as increasing demand raises the prices of the agricultural raw materials necessary to produce ethanol, namely corn, in the case of corn ethanol, or sugarcane in the case of sugar ethanol. This increasing demand means that the price of corn (or sugarcane) will rise, as increasing demand leads to increasing prices. While it's true that most of the world's corn production is not geared towards food consumption, one fourth of the world's population—some 1. 7 billion people—depend on corn for their daily survival.[22] The typical Mexican, for example, eats upwards of ten tortillas a day, so when the price of corn rises, he or she has to either spend less on other goods, or consume less corn (and depending on their income, less overall).[23]

However, biofuels such as ethanol don't merely raise food prices and cause ecological destruction directly; they also have the dubious distinction of doing both these things indirectly. The culprit is not simply that more corn, sugar and vegetable oils are being shifted from food consumption to fuel production; the problem is also that as these crops become more financially lucrative, an increasing number of farmers make the economically rational choice to stop growing whatever they were growing and to start growing corn or sugar cane. For example, a potato farmer, when faced with a flat price for potatoes and a rising price for corn, may make the decision to shift from planting potatoes to planting corn. However, since the potatoes were meant for food consumption and the corn is merely being processed into fuel, this effectively means that there is now less food to go around. Since the number of people to feed in the world increases every year, decreasing food is not something we should be doing.

As we have already seen in the fashion chapter, many farmers have shifted from growing food to growing the more financially lucrative cotton, a behavior that is paralleled in many locations when it comes to corn. In the Mexican state of Jalisco, corn farmers were once pitied because they were barely able to eke out a living because corn prices were so low. Now, however, things are so good that their fellow agave farmers are shifting gears to join the lucrative corn game, as one quarter of agave farmers are burning their fields to eliminate the blue hued cactus that forms the base of tequila, to make way for corn fields. These are the same agave fields that the United Nations Educational, Scientific and Cultural Organization (UNESCO) found so unique and irreparably intertwined with Mexican identity that they chose to label them a World Heritage site, a designation that declares a place to be of important cultural or physical significance.[24] While one could argue about the dubious need for tequila, this is not really about agave farmers, but rather about the palpable loss that occurs when we distort agricultural markets to raise food for fuel.

All of this is not mere economic supposition; we are already seeing the deleterious effects of ethanol consumption occurring on a global level. Over the past five years, global corn prices have consistently risen. The World Bank's food price index increased by 15 percent between October 2010 and January 2011, and in February 2011, the United States experienced its largest single month food increase in 36 years.[25] While it is true that some of this price surge is related not to ethanol production but rather to an increasing global consumption for meat (and thus the need for corn-based animal feed) by nations such as China, the role of ethanol cannot be ignored in this spike in food prices because over the same time period, the demand for corn-based ethanol has also grown. In 2005, US ethanol production stood at a mere 1 billion gallons; by 2006, when the effects of The Volumetric Ethanol Excise Tax Credit (VEETC), a policy created in 2004 to subsidize the production of ethanol in the United States, had taken full effect, ethanol production had quintupled to five billion gallons—some *forty* percent of US corn supplies now go not to feeding the world (or the world's animals) but to making fuel.[26] By 2009, that number had more than doubled again, topping some ten billion gallons.[27] The Paris-based Organization for Economic

Cooperation and Development and the UN's Food and Agriculture Organization expect biofuels to absorb 13 percent of global coarse grain production, 15 percent of vegetable oil and some 30 percent of sugar by 2020—an across the board increase from the previous decade.[28] Sarah Best, Oxfam's policy adviser on low carbon development, perhaps states it best, ""As more food stocks go into gas tanks, not stomachs, you have higher prices."[29]

The only way to change this situation is to either press natural ecosystems that are not currently being used into service to replace crops that are lost due to the planting of biofuels—a nightmare scenario we've already touched upon in the case of palm oil in Southeast Asia—or to simply refrain from using biofuels. Not all biofuels are created equal, however. Biodiesel made from waste vegetable oil—that is the oil that remains after cooking—mostly lives up to its green reputation, mainly, because it's the reuse of a waste product. In the United States, we consume an average of roughly 116 pounds per person per year, or roughly 15 gallons of oil per year.[30] When you consider that only a fraction of that is harvestable for conversion into biodiesel and that according to the United States Energy Information Administration, the average American uses 3 gallons of fuel oil *per day*, it's not likely that waste vegetable oil based biodiesel can meet our current energy requirements.[31]

Perhaps the most damning evidence on biofuel comes from Brazil. The country most made famous for waxes, samba, the Amazon and gorgeous beaches has, as we touched upon earlier, since the 1970's embarked upon a campaign for complete energy independence in part by heavily pursuing sugarcane ethanol. Yet, despite the fact that sugarcane ethanol is by most calculations the most energy efficient form of ethanol, and despite the fact that the Brazilian government has poured millions in research and support behind it, the country is still heavily dependent on oil. According to the *Oil and Gas Journal*, Brazil's oil consumption averaged 2.52 million barrels of oil per day, a number that has remained mostly flat over the years.[32] Ethanol has not stopping

Brazil from consuming oil, only from increasing that consumption. Yet, to merely maintain the status quo, Brazil has invested so much into something with a dubious environmental and sociological benefit, especially when you consider the existence of other infinitely more ecologically and economically equitable alternatives. It's just harder for industry to profit from those.

9. ENERGY ALTERNATIVES

The use of solar energy has not been opened up because the oil industry does not own the sun.—Ralph Nader

Polish comes from the cities; wisdom from the desert.
—Frank Herbert

With upright branches springing off of a central trunk not unlike arms brought together with hands and fingers held apart, as though awaiting a signal from on high, it's easy to imagine what the first group of Mormon settlers who crossed the Mojave Desert in the mid-nineteenth century must have seen when they renamed *yucca brevifolia* the Joshua tree after a biblical story in which Joshua reaches his hands up to the sky in prayer.[1] Native to North America and residing exclusively within the Mojave Desert, the Joshua tree is so iconic, so utterly American, that the Irish rock band U2 named their 1987 album, an album inspired by the band's "great romance" with the United States, after it.[2] These days, however, the Joshua tree, and its desert home, stand more as a symbol of the current state of American environmentalism: iconic, stoic and imperiled.

Deserts with their crushing stillness, aridity and seemingly glacial pace of change tend to evoke in most of us a deep sense of unease. In movies, deserts are rarely seen as places of wonder but rather are used to illustrate difficulty, hardship, and a fundamental sense of despair such as in the post-apocalyptical *Mad Max* films, the messianic sci-fi thriller *Dune*, and even in the *Star Wars* pictures. While popular culture seems to revel in the beauty of lush pastoral grasslands and is awed by mountains and seascapes, deserts by contrast are perennially cloaked in fear and contempt. In fact the word desert comes from the Latin word dēserere, meaning to abandon or forsake.[3] Our limited deviation from the trope of deserts as barren ecosystems with no redeeming qualities is in the realm of human spiritual development. Deserts are places that bring us so close to death that, if we survive, we usually emerge deeply spiritually transformed. After all, Jesus didn't spend 40 days and 40 nights in the rainforest. Yet even this sole redeeming quality of the desert is dependent on our belief in its unrelenting harshness.

During the 1840s, prospectors from the east traversed the Mojave's lowest, driest, and hottest valley, where summer temperatures that routinely top 120 degrees Fahrenheit, en route to the American gold mines in the west. They were the ones who gave the valley its macabre name of "death."[4] More than a century later, the term Death Valley has stuck. It is true that the valley's sometimes intense heat—its record temperature of 134 degrees Fahrenheit set in 1902 is a mere two degrees shy of the world record of 136 degrees Fahrenheit recorded in 1922 in Al 'Aziziyah, Libya—can kill a person if they are not careful. However, deserts, even Death Valley, are not ecological wastelands. If one knows how to look, deserts teem with life.[5]

In fact, for at least a thousand years, the Native American tribe, the Timbisha—a word meaning "Red Rock Face Paint"—have called not just the Mojave, but specifically Death Valley, home.[6] They have been able to do so because although the Mojave is not the lush, verdant landscape those of us who grew up in moister biomes are accustomed to, it does have life. Bird species such as cactus wren, mourning dove, quails and roadrunners can be found in the Mojave throughout the year, while migratory species such as the American robin and the western kingbird make the Mojave their seasonal home. It was not too long ago that jackrabbits and bighorn sheep provided plenty of game. At night, bats, owls, and mountain lions emerge.[7]

Our belief in the desert's barrenness has, ironically been its best protection from human encroachment. Dense human settlements require lots of water, a resource that deserts by definition lack. Even today, in the United States, desert cities though more common thanks to technological advances, are still relatively rare. Many of those that do exist such as Las Vegas and Phoenix often began as oases or places were water was in relative abundance. However, the abundance of another vital resource, in fact the one that makes deserts difficult to live in the first place, is now imperiling this delicate ecosystem. Over the past few years, investors, Silicon Valley-backed startups, and utility companies have become determined to harvest from the desert its most abundant resource, one that is not only infinitely renewable, but clean to boot—the sun. Little known companies like NextEra Energy, as well as utility giants like Pacific Gas & Electric and banks such as Goldman Sachs have filed dozens of applications to build massive solar arrays—row after row of solar panels linked together into a central power grid—on some three hundred thousand acres of currently undeveloped federal land. These permits were drawn not only in the Mojave Desert, but on land across the desert southwest, into Arizona's Sonoran Desert as well as the Chihuahuan Desert, which extends into parts of Texas, New Mexico and southeastern Arizona.[8] At the center of what some are calling the west's new gold rush is a deal between Pacific Gas and Electric and BrightSource Energy to build a 1,300 megawatt solar array—enough electricity to power approximately 845,000 homes.[9] Its first project is the Ivanpah Solar Electric Generating System, a 392 megawatt solar complex to be built in the Mojave Desert that once constructed will be arguably the world's largest solar array.[10]

Since at least the heady oil crisis period of the 1970s, we have been told that solar is the energy of the future. On April 18, 1977 then President Jimmy Carter delivered a televised speech on energy policy stating,

> Because we are now running out of gas and oil, we must prepare quickly for a...change, to strict conservation and to the use of coal and permanent renewable energy sources, **like solar power** (emphasis added).[11]

Clean, easy to store (unlike wind), and free of carbon emissions, solar energy's biggest handicap has been the sun itself, as the places best suited for solar energy generation (i.e. the sunniest climates) are often not the same places where the energy is needed. It's nearly impossible, for example, to generate enough solar energy locally to cover the needs of the misty city of Bellingham, Washington (population 80,000), which gets 227 days of cloud cover each year. At the same time, however, solar energy also works best—generates the most electricity—not when solar panels work individually, but rather when many solar panels are clustered together into sets known as arrays. The problem with this, however, is scale.

Take for example the city of Los Angeles, whose whopping annual average of 329 sunny days makes it seemingly the perfect candidate for onsite solar generation. That is until you look at how much energy the city uses. It's roughly 4 million inhabitants use 6,165 megawatts of electricity *every day* to power their cell phones, computers, air conditioners, telephones, and yes, electric cars. By contrast, one of the world's largest solar arrays, a 150 acre solar power plant built by General Electric in the town of Serpa, Portugal,124 miles southeast of Lisbon, generates 11 megawatts or .17 percent of the total amount of electricity Los Angeles uses daily. If the City of Angels, which is comprised of roughly 300,000 acres, wanted to generate all of its electricity via locally generated solar, it would require 84,000 acres or roughly a quarter of the city's land, to do so.[12]

Further, cities rarely provide ideal solar generation, as buildings obscure the panels blocking the sun's rays, thus inhibiting peak energy generation. By contrast, in the desert, solar power stations can mount their solar panels on movable bases that allow the panels to move with the sun and better capture its energy. It is into this landscape that generating solar in the desert and sending it into the cities can seem like an ideal proposition. One study has shown, for example, that solar panels placed in the Sahara could provide enough electricity to power all of Europe.[13]

Yet, much like that all that glitters isn't gold, when it comes to solar, all that's carbon-free is not inherently green. The panels themselves come with a long list of potential negative environmental impacts, some known and some we're still in the process of understanding. For example, although the energy created by solar panels doesn't generate carbon emissions, the process by which the panels are produced does. The production of silicon-based solar panels releases a gas called sulfur hexafluoride (SF6), the most potent greenhouse gas known to science.[14] According to the Intergovernmental Panel on Climate Change, over a 100 year period, SF6 has a global warming potential of 22,200 times that of CO2. In addition, there are a litany of hazardous compounds used or created as a byproduct of the fabrication of solar panels, including aerosolized silicon dust, the fairly toxic, highly combustible silane gas, the harmful to plant life sulfur dioxide, and trichloroethane, a compound that has been linked to all sorts of health problems, including cranial nerve damage and non-Hodgkin lymphoma in populations exposed to it via their drinking water.[15]

In Gaolong, China, the byproducts of energy firms that make polycrystalline silicon, also called polysilicon, a key component of solar panels, are destroying the local environment. Silicon tetrachloride, a waste product of the production of polysilicon, is highly toxic and yet a ubiquitous part of polysilicon fabrication.

For each ton of polysilicon produced, the process generates at least four tons of silicon tetrachloride liquid waste, which when exposed to humid air forms into poisonous hydrogen chloride gas. "The land where you dump or bury it will be infertile. No grass or trees will grow in the place. . . . It is like dynamite—it is poisonous, it is polluting. Human beings can never touch it," said Ren Bingyan, a professor at the School of Material Sciences at Hebei Industrial University, in a 2008 *Washington Post* article.[16] In developed nations, most companies are required to recycle polysilicon back into the manufacturing process, but because of cost and lack of oversight, Chinese companies often go the cheaper and easier route and illegally dump the substance, killing the soil and tainting surrounding groundwater.

And it's not just the manufacture of solar panels that's problematic; swathing the desert in solar panels is not without its costs, either. Across the American desert west, solar power plant projects have been delayed as local advocates challenge their impact on water resources, rare animals such as the desert tortoise and the kangaroo mouse, and plants such as the Mojave milkweed and the iconic Joshua Tree, that inhabit an extremely fragile ecosystem.[17] In 2009, the Berkeley-based Solar Millennium revealed that the plan for its Amargosa Farm Road Solar Project, located in Nye County, Nevada, would consume as much as 1.3 billion gallons of water per year or 20 percent of the desert valley's available water.[18] Solar power plants often use water in a process known as wet cooling to keep the power plants from overheating. The alternative is a process known as dry cooling, which uses fans and heat exchanges to prevent overheating, consuming less water but consuming extra electricity, which adds to costs and reduces efficiency.[19]

Further, locating solar power plants far from cities has the negative effect of reducing energy generation efficiency. The high tension wires needed to transport energy from the desert areas, where the solar energy is generated, to the cities where it is consumed, use between 7 and 8 percent of the electricity generated. Stated differently, roughly 8 percent of the energy generated simply gets lost en route. The need for such large, transmission lines, looping across tens of thousands of miles of isolated back country, also has the unintended consequence of causing wildfires. The wires break, sparking fires that rapidly spiral out of control before firefighters can reach them. And it's not just the wires themselves that cause the fires. The 1.9 billion dollar Sunrise Powerlink, a high-voltage power transmission line bringing 1000 megawatts of clean energy (a mix of solar and wind) from the Imperial Valley, home of the Algodones dunes (where scenes for Return of the Jedi were shot), to San Diego has been found to increase wildfire risk not just because of the transmission lines, but also because the maintenance roads for the lines opens up new areas for campers to smoke or light campfires.[20] The ideal locations for solar arrays, from an ecological perspective, are the sites of abandoned farms and ranches were the land is already degraded. Those locations, however, aren't always big enough or properly sited, to meet the needs of good solar generation.

These issues, of course, are not limited only to solar, as all transmission lines lose power over large distances, and pose some wildfire risk. But by creating roads to build solar arrays, and putting in roads to go with the new transmission lines, solar increases those risks. Perhaps most egregiously, we know that centralized electrical systems of this nature are problematic. Yet instead of thoughtfully pausing to consider how best to circumvent the problems we know exist, we are instead plowing ahead, eager to plug solar into a system riddled with known errors.

And then there is what is best described as the "Rumsfeld" problem. In February of 2002, then Secretary of Defense Donald Rumsfeld infamously stated,

> [T]here are known knowns; there are things we know we know. We also know there are known unknowns; that is

> to say we know there are some things we do not know. But there are also unknown unknowns—the ones we don't know we don't know.

Rumsfeld was talking about the Iraq War, but he could have just as easily been speaking about the wisdom of hijacking an ecosystem for our own well being, something we've done repeatedly in the past. Over the past 200 years, we have filled, flooded, drained, dredged, leveled and otherwise destroyed wetlands to build cities, farms, suburbs, and in the case of Florida's Disneyworld, an amusement park. Only after we created all of this destruction, however, did we recognize their value as hurricane buffers, carbon sinks, and as a vital component of the water cycle. As a result of our environmental shortsightedness, we are now spending billions of dollars on restoring wetlands.[22] We don't yet know if deserts play an equally vital, though different role in our ecosystems.

Solar energy is not the only alternative energy source that has significant downsides along with its carbon reducing upsides. For example, it has long been recognized that hydroelectric dams flood ecosystems, change river flows, cause downstream habitats to decline, and fundamentally change habitat conditions for fish and wildlife, leading to the erosion of diverse fish populations such as salmon in the Pacific Northwest. At least, we thought, they don't contributeto climate change. Increasingly, we're discovering that this supposition may be wrong. The forests flooded to create hydroelectric dams result in plant matter settling on the reservoir bottom, decomposing without oxygen and resulting in a build-up of dissolved methane.[23] The methane is then released into the atmosphere when the water passes through the damns turbines. (Recall, that the effect of methane on global warming is 21 times stronger than that of carbon dioxide.[24]) There is also increasing evidence that the underwater noise generated by tidal-power schemes—power stations which generate electricity from waves—negatively impacts marine species such as whales, seals, dolphins and certain species of fish that use underwater sounds for communication, navigation, and to find food.[25]

Ultimately, the issue is not that solar power, or wind, or geothermal, or wave, or any of the numerous green energy technologies that seem to emerge daily, are inherently bad. The point is that all of them—even the ones that are truly carbon neutral—have very real and potentially very harmful ecological costs. If you're the kangaroo rat, or the Mojave Desert tortoise, or any one of the species whose habitat is already threatened, you wouldn't particularly care that the development that drove you to extinction was "green." We need to acknowledge and respect those costs. Furthermore, most of the negative effects seem to be associated with the question of scale—it's the wide scale application of these energies that's potentially damaging. If, after all, Los Angeles could generate all of its electricity needs by simply placing solar panels atop existing buildings solar, it would be a lot greener. But unfortunately it can't—because we consume an ever increasing amount of electricity. The US Department of Energy (DOE) predicts that by 2025, we will consume 50 percent more electricity than we did in 2003.[26]

Can we even generate enough renewable energy to replace fossil fuel based energy without altering our current energy use patterns? According to Tad W. Patzek of the University of Texas at Austin and David Pimentel of Cornell University, the answer is no. In a March 2005 article published in *Critical Reviews in Plant Sciences* they wrote, "We want to be very clear: solar cells, wind turbines, and biomass-for-energy plantations can never replace even a small fraction of the highly reliable, 24-hours-a-day, 365-days-a-year, nuclear, fossil, and hydroelectric power stations. Claims to the contrary are popular, but irresponsible."[27] In short, alternative energy can meet our needs, but not our greed.

One of the more optimistic studies regarding our ability to power our future with renewable energies was produced by Greenpeace International and the European Renewable Energy Council, which argues that renewable energy sources could meet all global energy needs by 2090. That assessment, however, is based on incorporating strict efficiency standards. In other words, we would have to reduce our energy load.[28] Their models predict that between 2020 and 2050 efficiency will grow eight fold. However, in a 2008 *Time Magazine* article, Michael Grunwald wrote that,

> This may sound too good to be true, but the U.S. has a renewable-energy resource that is perfectly clean, remarkably cheap, surprisingly abundant and immediately available. It has astounding potential to reduce the carbon emissions that threaten our planet, the dependence on foreign oil that threatens our security and the energy costs that threaten our wallets. Unlike coal and petroleum, it doesn't pollute; unlike solar and wind, it doesn't depend on the weather; unlike ethanol, it doesn't accelerate deforestation or inflate food prices; unlike nuclear plants, it doesn't raise uncomfortable questions about meltdowns or terrorist attacks or radioactive-waste storage, and it doesn't take a decade to build...This miracle juice goes by the distinctly boring name of energy efficiency...[29]

And yet even these reassurances ring hollow, as we have been increasing household energy efficiency since the 1970s—yet our household energy bills have remained the same while our per capita energy use has gone up. What gives? Energy efficiency and energy conservation, although often used interchangeably, are not the same thing. Energy efficiency is using less energy to provide the same level of service—it's increasing the miles per gallon of a vehicle, reducing the amount of electricity needed to run a refrigerator, or reducing the amount of fuel needed to heat a home. In theory, increasing a product's energy efficiency would reduce the amount of energy we consume. In practice, that hasn't been the case. As I touched on in the housing chapter, we've eroded many of the efficiencies gained through improved insulation and better heaters in housing by simply building bigger houses. We have eroded the savings of increased fuel efficiency in cars by driving further. And we have eliminated the efficiency gains of our appliances by simply purchasing more of them.

Take the humble household refrigerator. While kitchen and laundry appliances account for roughly one-third of household electricity use, more electricity is used for refrigerators than for space heating, water heating, or lighting.[30] In short, refrigerators use a lot of energy. A 2010 report by the World Economic Forum and IHS Cambridge Energy Research Associates found that while the average American refrigerator now uses three-fourths less energy than the average refrigerator from 1975—despite being 20 percent larger—Americans are eroding the energy savings gained from efficiency by holding onto their old, inefficient refrigerators.[31] Rather than replacing them, people are pressing their older refrigerators into service in other parts of their homes. One fourth of American households now have a second refrigerator, a number that is steadily increasing at the rate of one percentage point per year. Removing the 29.6 million secondary refrigerator units nationwide would save 25 million megawatt hours, roughly equivalent to 2.8 billion dollars.[32]

And it's not just refrigerators. For example, the average air conditioner manufactured today can be from 20 to 40 percent more energy efficient than an air conditioner made ten years ago. The United States, according to scientist Stan Cox, author of *Losing Our Cool: Uncomfortable Truths About Our Air-Conditioned World*, consumes roughly half a trillion kilowatts per year just to air condition its homes and offices.[33] To put that into context, this is the entire electricity consumption of all sixty nations of the continent of Africa. The idea that "efficiency" can reduce this number is laughable, given that much of the problem is that more of us are using air conditioning than ever before, in part because air conditioning actually makes the surrounding area hotter, chilling indoor air while sucking out hot air, resulting in the aforementioned heat island effect. Stated more plainly, using air conditioning forces us to use still more air conditioning. It is no wonder that our energy consumption, economic crises aside, seems to be heading in only one direction—up.

What we need—and what we're unwilling to discuss at any length—is energy *conservation*. Although energy conservation, or the reduction in our use of energy, can be brought about with energy efficiency (if, for example, we built more efficient homes, but didn't build bigger ones), they are not the same thing. We conserve energy when we turn on the lights as we leave the room. We conserve energy when we eschew driving to the supermarket for walking or cycling. We conserve energy when we take President Jimmy Carter's famously lampooned advice and turn down the thermostat a few degrees and slip on a sweater. In other words, we conserve energy when we deliberately consume less. A 2011 study by scientists at Finland's Aalto University, which used a brand new hybrid lifecycle analysis approach to quantify carbon emissions, in part by allocating emissions to who consumes a finished product rather than to who and where the product is produced, found that how much carbon emissions one generates is dependent upon how many goods and services one consumes.[34] Jukka Heinonen, one of the researchers on the study, said, "If a TV set is made in a factory in the countryside but bought and used by a person in a town, the carbon emission generated from making the television should be allocated to the consumer, not to a manufacturer making it for the consumer."

The less energy that we consume the fewer windmills that we have to erect, the fewer solar arrays we have to introduce into a delicate ecosystem, the fewer ecological tradeoffs that we have to make. Alternative energy sources, though often greener than the technologies they seek to replace, are not without a cost. The only way to mitigate that cost is to use less of them.

PART III—THE WAY FORWARD

10. OUR CONSUMPTION PROBLEM

> *Consumer identity has replaced actual character building. Why be that person when you can just appropriate the accoutrements?*—Internet Commenter

> *We used to build civilizations. Now we build shopping malls.*—Bill Bryson

> *A thing is right when it tends to preserve the integrity, stability and beauty of the biotic community. It is wrong when it tends otherwise.*—Aldo Leopold

At the core of our environmental crisis is what I like to refer to as the "IKEA Effect." On the surface, IKEA is an excellent example of a company that exhibits—or at least tries to exhibit—sustainable practices. For example, IKEA phased out the use of polyvinyl chloride (PVC) when the idea of doing so wasn't even a twinkle in the eyes of most other retailers. They also clearly list the renewable and recyclable components of their products on their website, allowing consumers to pick items made with renewable materials. And they do all of this while offering low prices, and awakening our collective consciousness to the idea that "affordable yet stylish" does not have to be an oxymoron.

At the same time, however, IKEA has also radically shifted how many of us view furniture—namely, that furniture is disposable. Because many of its products are manufactured not from wood but from less durable, less reparable wood composites such as particle board, we tend to cycle through IKEA products fairly quickly.[1] When we get bored with what we have, we simply go out and buy a new one. Similarly, when products we buy at IKEA break, we don't try to repair them—we just buy new ones. This is not limited to IKEA—Target, Wal-Mart and a host of other retailers have gotten us on the buy-use-dispose treadmill. In fact, according to author Paul Hawken, when you step back and look at the total consumption system—sourcing (mining, harvesting, extraction), manufacture (processing, fabrication), transport and use, a mere *one percent*—is still in use six months after the cycle began.[2] We use a tremendous amount of resources, and do irreparable harm to the planet, to fabricate stuff that exists for only the briefest moment before we simply throw it out. We consume resources at rates faster than they can repair themselves, a practice that is inherently unsustainable regardless of how you slice it.

The rise of the IKEA mentality—a mix of instant gratification with the veneer of style and sustainability, while at its core utterly disposable and unsustainable—can be seen in the stop gap measures we undertake in the name of sustainable development. At its best, when it's put forward by companies such as Patagonia, who have a true commitment to sustainability and who take a holistic view of what they are producing and their role in the landscape, green purchasing can be a step on the journey which we as a collective society need to take in order to fundamentally shift the way we view ourselves, our notion of work, and our economic and social systems, if we are to change our current model of overconsumption.

But that is not how green consumption is positioned in the marketplace. Too many businesses and environmental groups have led us to believe that if we buy the correct collection of products, we can save the planet. While these assurances have done much to assuage our collective guilt, and even more to create a generation of smug eco-shoppers, it has done next to nothing to fundamentally change the environmental landscape, while in many cases actively contributing to environmental degradation and misinformation. By positioning environmental sustainability as a market choice, akin to choosing between a whip and a no whip latte, we downgrade the urgency of our current ecological situation. The ecosystem in which human beings and human society has managed to successfully evolve is rapidly changing in drastic ways which are directly tied to our overconsumption. Yet, we've managed to weigh the gravity of this cultural and ecological destruction into the same formula as cost, appearance, and durability.

Winnowing itself through this tale of consumption, of what it means to buy green, is this one simple truth: purchasing green can be good, but buying less is better. This simple truism is the key to unlocking the door on our future sustainability. For example, the study by researchers at Aalto University in Finland that was referred to in the previous chapter, in which the environmental impacts of products were assigned to the end consumer as opposed to the producer, showed that, more than anything else, an individual's climate impact via the CO2 emissions they cause to be emitted is related to how many goods and services they consume.[3] Whether we're talking about energy, clothes, food, or shelter, the sheer volume and pace of our consumption is the root problem. This is not to say one shouldn't purchase sustainably made things. Buying, for example, a dresser made from reclaimed wood or sustainably logged wood, is better than buying a cheaply made one—but only if you intend to hold onto that dresser for awhile, and not purchase a new one in two or three years. The bottom line is that we have to consume less. That we have such trouble recognizing this is not because there isn't a problem, but rather because the lens through which we view the world has become distorted.

To see this distortion first hand, one merely needs to watch some of the more popular shows currently on TV. Stacks of newspaper's dating back to the Vietnam era, towers of depleted toilet paper rolls, and massive bundles of flattened soda cans are just some of the prized possessions of the those who appear on the hit A&E show *Hoarders*, which is billed as an inside look into the lives of people whose inability to part with their belongings is so out of control that they are on the verge of a personal crisis. Competitor network TLC has emerged with its own version, *Hoarding: Buried Alive*. Americans, it seems, can't get enough of this voyeuristic window into a world of people literally drowning in stuff: the pet hoarder who has dozens of dead cats interspersed amongst the living ones; the man for whom even a worn bathroom sponge is a prized possession; living rooms filled with enough random tchotkes to rival any dusty, dimly lit thrift shop; kitchens brimming with filled trash bags; counters sagging under the combined waste of rusted and riddled pots and pans; food encrusted plates and bowls, with enough silverware to outfit a brigade. What's most shocking are the things that have never been used in the first place—outfits hanging in closets with tags still on them, electronics still in their original packaging, unused Christmas decorations.

"We're not like them," we reassure ourselves as we watch these people for entertainment, despite the fact that we load our homes with stuff and cram the spillover into garages or backyard storages sheds. When that gets too cumbersome, we move, renting or buying bigger spaces, bigger palaces to house our stuff. If that's not an option, we cart our stuff to one of the 46,000 self-storage facilities, covering one billion square feet of storage space, spread across America's urban fringes and rural roads before, finally, we give up and donate the salvageable materials to charity and simply throw the rest away.[4] That trash, if it doesn't end up in our oceans, rivers, and streams, ends up in landfills.

What separates us from our hoarding cousins is not that we don't buy far too much stuff, but that most of us still have the ability to get rid of at least some of it. We are not faced with the dizzying volume of our consumption on an everyday basis. As the Seattle based photographer Chris Jordan, famous for photographing garbage in a way that helps to depict the scale of things that we consume and discard, said:

> "The problem is this cumulative effect from the behaviors of hundreds of millions of individuals. Each person looks around at his or her own behavior, and it doesn't look all that bad. What we each have to expand our consciousness to hold is that the cumulative effect of hundreds of millions of individual consumer decisions is causing the worldwide destruction of our environment. The hard part of that is the notion of the enormity of the collective...So, the only way we know about the staggering effects we're having on our environment, for example, is to read scientific reports about statistics, but there's no where you can actually go and see the numbers. The only way we have of relating to these incredibly important facts about our mass consumption is statistics. And the problem with statistics is they're so dry and emotionless. If we're going to be motivated as a culture to change our behavior, then we're going to have to find a deep motivation."[5]

It takes a tremendous amount of energy, of resources, to make our stuff—even those labeled green—and that energy is not reflected in the way we rapidly use and discard our material goods. According to the EPA, we generate an average of 250 million tons of trash per year, roughly eight hundred and fourteen pounds of trash per person.[6] That's approximately the same weight as twenty average sized eleven year olds. And that's only municipal waste, the stuff we throw out that goes through government channels—it doesn't calculate private business and industrial waste. Conservative estimates say that municipal waste is 20 percent of the total reported waste stream. In truth, if you were to tally all of our personal consumption, it would amount to a mere 25 percent of global resource use, as business, industry and agriculture account for the other 75 percent.[7] Every year, the private sector throws out an additional *billion* tons of waste. To fully grasp the scale of our consumption try visualizing this: before New York City's Fresh Kills Landfill was closed in 2001 and masked with a layer of soil and grass as part of a plan to turn the area into a community park, the sprawling landfill had managed in a mere 55 years to span some 2,200 acres and reach a height of 225 feet. Fresh Kills was taller than the Statue of Liberty.

All of this shows how we consume more than we need to, more than we have to, and perhaps, more than we'd like to. For example, the meat we purchase at our local supermarket, enclosed on a foam tray, wrapped in plastic, and then put in a plastic bag before being double bagged with the rest of our groceries, represents an order of magnitude of consumption never before seen in human history. Once upon a time, that same purchase would have been wrapped in butcher's paper before being tucked into a tote or maybe a paper bag. Not that this was necessarily ideal, but we've replaced a cycle that was at least biodegradable and based on renewable resources with one dependent on layers upon layers of non-renewable resources that will house our food for but the smallest moment, and yet endure in our ecosystems for an untold number of years. In the face of this, hauling our canvas tote bag to the supermarket is not going to solve the problem.

This kind of massive, passive, consumption is made worse by our deliberate overconsumption. Take the television set. According to the audience measurement company Nielsen, in 2009 the average American home had 2.93 TV sets, a 21 percent increase from 2000, when the average American home had 2.43 sets, and 47 percent higher than in 1990, when the average home had 2 television sets.[8] The average of 2.86 TV sets stands in counterbalance to the fact that the average household in 2009 contained only 2.5 people. In your typical household today, we have more television sets than people. And, we've managed to increase the number of televisions even as the number of computers (and our ability to watch television programming on them) has increased, as has the number of smart phones, tablet computers, and mp3 players, all of which allow us to watch televised programming.

The television set is a great analogy for our consumption because they're expensive, resource intensive, durable goods whose use is driven less by need then by the perception of need. For example, in 1998, roughly 12 million cathode-ray television sets were thrown out. CRT's are the bulkier, old-school sets that most of us associate with the traditional concept of "television." They are also toxic soups of lead, cadmium, mercury and other heavy metals. They are the kinds of goods that one should hold onto for a very long time, and in a perfect world, the parts would be recycled (in truth, less than 15 percent of television sets are recycled).[9] By 2005, more than 20 million CRT television sets were thrown out, while by 2008, that number had blossomed to 24 million. In less than a decade, the number of television sets that were making their way to the waste stream—many of them still perfectly functioning—had doubled.

Why are we suddenly throwing out our televisions? Given that television ownership has increased over the past decade, it's not that we all suddenly decided to go TV free. The likely answer is the rise of digital, and more specifically, LCD flat screen televisions. Suddenly we no longer had to have big bulky TV's in our homes, but instead could own television sets so sleek we could hang them on the wall, like art, hiding them behind sliding pictures when not in use. As a result, millions of us tossed out perfectly functional CRT television sets for a technological upgrade that for all intents and purposes was not functionally different from that which it replaced. It was also an environmental downgrade. The EPA's Design for the Environment Program did an environmental life-cycle assessment of CRT versus LDC screens and found that out of sixteen environmental impact categories, LCD's fared worse in every category but energy use. [10]

However, because many people chose to purchase significantly larger LCD televisions, total energy use has still gone up. In addition, CRT televisions had a lifespan on average double that of the current crop of flat screen televisions and were far easier (though not necessarily cheap) to repair, thus extending their lives still further. Put simply, we've thrown out millions of perfectly good, or easily reparable television sets and replaced them with a more environmentally toxic, resource intensive product with a shorter life span.[11]

It's not just TV's, but shoes, jeans, food, vacations—we live in a culture in which an almost silent beat compels us to consume, consume, and then to consume some more. After the attacks on September 11th, 2001, then President George W. Bush famously told us that the best thing we could do for our nation was to "go shopping." And boy do we shop. We spend up to a quarter of our leisure time, nearly hour a day, shopping.[12] On vacation, our preferred activity is to shop some more. The average American is no longer referred to as a person or a citizen but rather as a consumer. Says Tim Jackson, the Economics Commissioner on the UK's Sustainable Development Commission: "this is a strange, rather perverse, story, just to put it in very simple terms. It's a story about us, people, being persuaded to spend money we don't have, on things we don't need, to create impressions that won't last, on people we don't care about."

This idea, to consume at all costs, even to our own detriment, is so ingrained in our culture that when people choose not to shop, we freak out. In the mid-eighties and again in the late nineties, the media was enamored by a small, but significant trend that it found unsettling: some people were choosing to consume less. The trend, alternatively called "simple living," "voluntary simplicity" or merely "downshifting" was chronicled in books such as Duane Elgin's *Voluntary Simplicity* and Juliet Schor's *The Overspent American*. These books followed the stories of an increasing number of Americans who, fed up with keeping up with the Joneses and the perennial rat race of increasing consumption, or simply the sheer volume of waste associated with modern living, were deliberately deciding to downsize—some would say violently so—their lives. And though the media became less enamored of them over time, they never did go away. After all, Jay Schaeffer of Tumbleweed Tiny Homes has to be selling his micro manses to *someone*.

These deliberate downsizers take on many forms. The most extreme are perhaps the freegans, a hodgepodge assembly of ideologies which mix radical environmentalism, anti-consumerism, and communism in one central manner: they buy almost nothing. Instead, the members of this movement troll dumpsters, salvage yards, and curbs on trash day to secure everything from furniture to food. Others take a more moderate approach, leaving stressful, financially successful jobs for employment with fewer hours and more time for leisure. They trade in large houses for much smaller homes or apartments, downsizing from two cars to one, or alternatively, going car free altogether. Both groups, and those who exist somewhere in the middle, are all motivated by one thing—a freedom from stuff. They take seriously the adage that "what you own, owns you" and have made a deliberate decision to limit both how much and the kinds of things they own.

That anyone would willingly, willfully choose to consume less in the very same country where houses have ballooned from no garage to two car garages—not as a place to store the second car but as a place to store additional stuff—seems to many to be crazily out of step. But increasingly, the evidence suggests that the traditional American way of life is the one that is out of step. If we want to save the planet, if we want to save ourselves, many of us have to consume, much, much less. However, in this country of not just plenty, but of *more*, it's hard for us to make peace with the concept of less. In January of 2011, the United States Department of Agriculture shocked the nation when it suggested, for the first time in its 21-year history of publishing its dietary guidelines, that Americans eat *less*. For two decades, the USDA had focused on telling Americans, a nation whose population has for years been physically decaying from the overconsumption of food, to eat *more*—more fruits, more vegetables, more whole grains, etc.—without ever pointing out that, armed with finite stomachs, to eat more of anything *healthy*, we had to eat less of the things that rendered us unhealthy. Less, you see, is not always a bad thing. Less can even be good.

In a truly sustainable world, we would consume nothing but biodynamic, fair trade, shade grown, bird friendly, locally roasted coffee, but we would also consume less of it. We would wear clothes sewn from fabrics made from locally grown, sustainably sourced materials, but we won't have quite so many pairs of pants, or dresses or shirts. We would walk or cycle or hop the tram to work, and live in small single family homes, or multi-storied homes fueled primarily by wind, solar or geothermal. In this paradigm, stuff would return to being just *stuff* and not symbolic ways of filling a void of low-self worth, of ego. The obvious question is, then, if consumption is our root problem, why aren't we dealing with it? We aren't challenging our consumption paradigm, quite simply, because our economy won't let us.

11. CRASH THE SYSTEM OR TRASH THE PLANET

> *Be glad that you're greedy; the national economy would collapse if you weren't.*—Mignon McLaughlin

> *Anyone who believes exponential growth can go on forever in a finite world is either a madman or an economist.*—Kenneth Boulding

> *The economy is a wholly owned subsidiary of the environment, not the reverse.*—Herman Daly

For most of us, who live with a significant buffer between our daily lives and the natural world, it can be easy to ignore the signs that something is amiss with the environment. We shrug off a cooler than normal spring as nothing but an annoyance—just a few extra weeks of bulky winter clothes. We learn that 13 of the highest average global temperatures have occurred in the 15 years since 1997 and we tuck that fact away in our mental file cabinet of items that while interesting, are not relevant to our day-to-day lives.[1] Massive floods in the Midwest threaten lives, crops, and homes, and yet we simply resign ourselves to paying higher prices for bread at the supermarket. Although it's impossible to draw a straight line between these—and many, many more—unusual weather events and global climate change, we do know that climate change both increases the frequency of storms and creates unusual weather events. At the very least, then, these events should be cause for pause. Instead, most of us treat them as tragic but discrete problems with little to no attention paid to their deeper causes.

Instead we seem to be perennially fixated on the economy. Of course, in many ways, this makes perfect sense, as we are still dealing with the fallout of the global, near economic collapse of 2008 and its slow recovery. Not only are millions of Americans still out of work or underemployed, but countless young people, fresh out of college and vocational programs and just embarking on their careers, have been unable to get the jobs necessary to actually start a career. The global economy seems to be hanging on by a skinny thread and there's a fear that another shock will unravel the whole thing and send us into the abyss. It's far easier to wrap one's head around the very personal ability to feed one's family, or pay one's bill in the short term, than to worry about an environmental catastrophe that seems a long ways away.

On the other hand, however, it's been more than forty years since the first Earth Day in 1970, four decades since we became collectively aware of the scale to which we are harming the planet—an awareness that is expanded upon regularly with new discoveries in environmental research. And yet, for those forty years we have continued to put the economy before the environment. The 2006 American Environmental Values Survey by ecoAmerica found that 77 percent of Americans say they worry about the environment. However, when asked how concerned they are about the environment in comparison to other issues such as terrorism, gasoline prices, the economy, and taxes, the environment doesn't even crack the top 20.[2] Further, 83 percent believe that we can achieve environmental protection and economic growth simultaneously—which may be why the idea of green jobs seems so compelling.

The delicious bit of irony is that the most significant reductions in US carbon emissions have come courtesy of the recent global economic recession. Stripped of credit, with less access to cash, global consumption dropped, and with it carbon emissions.

According to the U.S. Energy Information Administration (EIA), energy related carbon dioxide emissions declined by 2.8 percent in 2008 and by a whopping 7 percent in 2009.[3] The 2009 decline was both the largest absolute and percentage decline since EIA started recording annual carbon data in 1949. While other factors influence carbon emissions levels, the economy is a key factor as the EIA points out: "… changes in emissions are highly correlated with economic activity."[4] In 2010, as the economy recovered, our carbon emissions also rebounded, growing by 3.9 percent.[5] All of this clearly points to the fact that it is the sheer size of our economic activity—i.e. our consumption—that is the root cause of not just our climate woes, but many of our environmental problems as well. Why then don't we do something about it?

We don't act because of one unsettling truth: if we were to make reducing our consumption to a level that was both materially satisfying and ecologically sustainable our central focus, our entire global economic system would collapse. This isn't a hyperbole. Our economic system is based on the need for perpetual growth; we either grow our economy or it dies, taking us along with it. The economy this year must be larger than it was last year; next year's economy has to be bigger than this year's. On average, the US economy, measured in Gross Domestic Product (GDP), must be 3.3 percent larger than the year before. According to a 2011 report by the consulting firm McKinsey and Company,

> A drop in the rate of GDP growth from its historic 50-year average of 3.3 percent per annum, to say 1.5 percent for each of the next 20 years would be more damaging to prosperity and jobs in the United States than even a double-dip recession sometime in the next 12 months. To deliver economic prosperity for this generation and the ones that follow, the United States needs to retool the economy's engine so that it can run at a higher sustainable growth rate for decades to come.[6]

The way in which the global economy is built on structured growth is not just a component—it's a necessity written into the very language the economy. When a person eats too much they gain weight, when they hit the treadmill a few times a week they lose weight. In the parlance of economics, however, a person would not "lose" weight, but would instead experience a weight "contraction," which implies that the form still retains its original content but simply occupies less space, or they would experience negative weight gain, implying that the goal is always to gain weight. Similarly, when our economy does not grow it experiences an economic contraction, or negative growth, which is always viewed as a temporary problem (an economic correction) that needs to be overcome. The country of Japan has been undergoing an economic contraction for roughly twenty years, in part because it's population has been decreasing (it's hard to consume more when you have fewer people), yet it still talks in the parlance of growth, with its economy being viewed as "in correction," instead of accepting the fact that what is has been experiencing for two decades and counting is likely a new normal.[7]

When an economy doesn't grow, we get what economists refer to as a recession. Specifically, a recession is a period of two consecutive quarters during which the economy shrinks.[8] Recessions affect the ability for people to find and keep jobs—during recessions unemployment rates rise. According to National Bureau of Economic Research data, there were 14 recessions between 1929 to 2001, the most famous of which was the Great Depression of 1929 (though less clearly defined than a recession, a deep, prolonged recession is called a depression). When the economy shrinks people suffer. The Great Depression, precipitated by the stock market crash on October 29, 1929, caused international trade to decline by more than 50 percent and left the United States with unemployment rates as high as 25 percent. The price of food plummeted more than 60 percent, kicking some farmers, unable to make their mortgage payments, off of their land, while other farmers left food literally rotting in the fields, even as many in the cities went hungry, because the cost of harvesting was higher than the price that could be fetched at market.[9]

Our solution to problems such as the Great Depression has been focused on finding a way to both expand and stabilize growth. In this vein, President John Kennedy once said that a rising tide—referring to the economy—lifts all boats. Increasingly, however, the evidence today suggests that many of those boats are leaking. In 2010, 46.2 million Americans—roughly one in six people—were living below the poverty line of $22,314 a year for a family of four.[10] The United States makes enough food to feed every single one of its residents, yet millions go hungry. In 2010, 17.2 million households or roughly one in seven were food insecure, meaning "their access to adequate food is limited by a lack of money and other resources."[11] Even more shocking is that one third of those households had "very low food security" which means that people in the household either consumed less or went without food (i.e. they were hungry) because they simply couldn't afford food.[12] Similarly, every year 3.5 million Americans experience homelessness—while at the same time 18.4 million, nearly 11 percent, of houses stand empty.[13]

These problems have grown worse over the past several decades, coinciding with a severe rise in the income gap. In 1975, the top 0.1 percent earned about 2.5 percent of the nation's income; by 2008 that number had *quadrupled* to 10.4 percent.[14] A 2007 MIT working paper titled "Inequality and Institutions in 20th Century America" shows that from 1980 to 2005 of the total increase in American's income, 80 percent went to the top one percent. In many cases, income to those at the top increased even as income to those in the middle and bottom decreased. The pie may be getting bigger, but most people's share of that pie is getting smaller. According to a 2011 report in *Mother Jones*, 10 percent of Americans control two-thirds of the country's net worth, with the top one percent controlling 35 percent.[15] According to the Central Intelligence Agency, income distribution in the United States is more unequal than in Cameroon, Guyana, Nicaragua, and Venezuela, roughly on par with Uruguay, Argentina, and Ecuador and just ahead of Uganda and Jamaica.[16] In his 1975 book *Equality and Efficiency*, economist Arthur M. Okun, former chairman of the Council of Economic Advisers, wrote that

> American society proclaims the worth of every human being. All citizens are guaranteed equal justice and equal political rights. Everyone has a pledge of speedy response from the fire department and access to national monuments. As American citizens, we are all members of the same club. Yet at the same time, our institutions say 'find a job or go hungry,' 'succeed or suffer'...They award prizes that allow the big winners to feed their pets better than the losers can feed their children.[17]

I want to make it clear that some income inequality within an economic system isn't inherently bad. If most doctors, for example, didn't earn more than most real estate brokers (who require less education), there would be less of an incentive for doctors to take on the years of schooling (and debt) that it requires to earn a medical degree. The issue in today's society is the scale of inequality. Large income inequalities are problematic for several reasons. First, they breed corruption, especially in democracies where wealth and political power are often more easily exchanged. As the wealthy get wealthier, it both increases their political influence (see Bush and Kennedy families) and allows them to support policies that make themselves wealthier at the expense of others. An example of this is the "Halliburton loophole" which is connected to former Vice President Dick Cheney, who had strong ties to the oil, gas, and military company Halliburton. The loophole prevents the Environmental Protection Agency from regulating the hydrofracking process, a method of extracting natural gas that has been shown to contaminate drinking water supplies with a number of toxic chemicals that are used in the process.[18] This loophole benefits the hydrofracking companies by allowing them to dig and sell natural gas without paying a price for their environmental destruction. At the same time, the ranchers and farmers who see their livelihoods disappear with the emergence of water so toxic it is sometimes flammable, suffer. However, under current law, there is nothing they can do about it.

Large income inequalities also limit social mobility. Contrary to our Horatio Alger mythos of people pulling themselves up by their bootstraps, according to a 2010 study on social mobility published by the Organization for Economic Cooperation and Development, the United States hovers near the bottom among industrialized nations for social mobility, or the ability for an individual to surpass the income level, socioeconomic class and educational attainment of their family.[19] To place this in context, Canada, France, Germany and most Scandinavian countries are each more socially mobile than the United States. And when people do try and move between classes in this country, they don't get very far. According to the Economic Mobility Project of the Pew Charitable Trusts, "More than 50 percent of individuals who start in the bottom will stay there ten years later."[20] The picture is not much rosier for those born into the middle class, as roughly 40 percent born there (with middle class defined as those falling between the 30th and 70th percentiles of income distribution) remaining there, while 33 percent move downward.[21] In the United States, the class you are born into, or the one below it, is the one in which you are most likely going to live, and die.

From hunger in the Great Depression to hunger in the 21st century, to the issues of social mobility and wealth inequity, the problem has never been lack of food, or lack of wealth. The issue has always been that the economic system was decoupled from the physical system—and people suffered as a result. This is the same problem with the economic system's growth paradigm in relation to the environment; we've decoupled our economic system from that of our environment, and the physical environment suffers as a result. For example, if human growth followed the American economy's required average rate of 3.3 percent annual expansion, your typical American male who stood at an average height of 70 inches, or roughly 5 feet 10 inches and weighed 155 pounds at age 18, would stand a towering 85 inches, or 7 feet 1 inch, by age 24. By the time this man was 30, he would be 8 feet 6 inches. By the time he retired at age 65, he would be almost 30 feet tall and weigh more than 700 pounds. This admittedly absurd example illustrates how insane and unsustainable our mandate of endless economic growth truly is—there are physical limits to growth that our economic system fails to acknowledge.

Before we go any further, let's be clear: this is not about a particular type of economic system, be it socialism, communism, or capitalism. When it comes to the environment, these systems are more similar than dissimilar because their focus is on who owns the means of production, and not why we're driven to produce in the first place. And none of these systems question the rationale behind our production. This explains why communist countries (with perhaps the exception of Cuba) have environmental track records no better than that of their capitalist counterparts. The Aral Sea disaster and the Chernobyl nuclear power plant meltdown each happened under communist regimes. In fact, each of these economic systems seem just as unaware as capitalist systems that the Earth is a finite planet with limited resources.

Any economic system we create is dependent on our limited planet for the resources that flow through it. In mathematics, we would say that the economy is a subset of the set we call Earth. Systems based on economic growth, however, tend to treat the planet as a subset of the set we call the economy. For the less mathematically inclined, a perhaps more visual analogy lies in the relationship between cows and milk. As we all know, milk comes from cows and can be turned into a variety of things, such as cream, cheese, ice cream, and yogurt. Ultimately, however, in order to get any of these wonderful products, we have to take care of the cow. If we focus too much on the milk and ignore its source, the cow dies and takes the milk with it. In this analogy, the planet is the cow and the economic system is the milk. We've become so focused on the economic system that we've forgotten that it's dependent on the planet.

To understand why perpetual economic growth isn't possible, let's look at the problem through the lens of simple, personal economics. Let's say you earn $1,000 dollars a month and have $10,000 in savings. If you spend exactly what you earn, you will never need tap into that savings. However, say you have to spend $1,500 one month due to some unforeseen costs. You would be able to do so by pulling $500 dollars from your savings. If this withdrawal is a onetime act, it's no big deal. If, however, you regularly spend $1,500 dollars a month because your expenses (car, apartment, food) exceed your salary, you're going to get into trouble very quickly—in just twenty months you will no longer be able to meet your financial needs. This economic example is akin to what we're doing ecologically to the planet.

As a whole, the Earth is a closed system. All of the resources at our disposal are located within the planet. Our only external input is the sun in the form of solar radiation. While things within our little terrarium may shift—some plants may grow more rapidly, others may die off—whatever is found within the system remains within the system. Within this closed system, broadly speaking, we have two types of resources: renewable and non-renewable. Renewable resources are those resources such as trees and water that, as the name implies, renew themselves. If we pick an apple from an apple tree, in a year, there will be more apples. If we chop down a tree, in a few decades another tree will grow to replace it.

The second category, non-renewable resources, includes resources that either won't come back after they are used, or ones that may actually renew themselves, but at a rate so slow it renders them nonrenewable for all intents and purposes. For example, it takes between 100 and 500 years to make a single cubic inch of topsoil—the very soil we depend upon to grow our crops so that we can feed ourselves. When we destroy topsoil through erosion, urbanization, or poor farming practices, the people who depend upon those crops are not likely to be around in 100 years to use the new stuff that nature will eventually create. Consequently, soil is considered a non-renewable resource. Similarly, fossil fuels such as natural gas and oil are the remains of plants and animals that lived up to 300 million years ago. The earth can at some point make more natural gas and oil, but not soon enough for us to immediately fill our tailpipe when we run out of gas on the expressway.

Ultimately, a society dependent upon non-renewable resources, especially one such as ours that depends *heavily* on them to provide everything including our most basic needs of food, shelter, and sanitation, is a society built on a quicksand. At some point—and a growing body of research indicates that we are reaching that point—we are going to run out of key resources. The Paris-based International Energy Agency (IEA) predicts that oil is rapidly running out with global oil production set to peak within the next ten years.[22] Several sources agree that fish stocks—at current rates of consumption—are on the precipice of collapse, with the world's oceans set to be depleted of fish by 2050.[23] Perhaps most frighteningly, a mix of ecosystem destruction and climate change is leading to a reduction in water supplies. In the United States, at least thirty states already have some kind of water stress, a situation expected to worsen as the climate heats up, not only causing droughts in the West but, due to an increasing number of storms taxing sewer systems, limiting water access on the East Coast as well.[24]

Despite these nightmare scenarios, these resources won't actually just disappear, but instead will become accessible to only the richest segments of our society. The rest of us, and many are already in this position, are going to have to make do with the waste of the ever dwindling masses of the super wealthy. For example, the majority of the world still does not ride in single passenger cars (never mind own one), doesn't eat meat on a daily basis—even when their dietary practices allow it—and most people have never and will never set foot in an airplane. A reduction in global fossil fuel supply means that those of us in the category of "rich" will soon enter into the category of "poor."

There is another, non-ecological, reason as to why we should approach this concept of perpetual economic growth with skepticism, and it lies within the very definition of an economic system, which is

> the structure of production, allocation of economic inputs, distribution of economic outputs, and consumption of goods and services in an economy. It is a set of institutions and their social relations. Alternatively, it is the set of principles by which problems of economics are addressed, such as the economic problem of *scarcity* through allocation of *finite* productive resources.[25](emphasis added)

How can we have the idea of an economic system which acknowledges that resources are scarce and finite and yet, at the same time, live within an actual economic system which ignores that these same limits exist? If we followed true logic of what an economic system is, our goal should be to live within the limits of our renewable resources. The problem with depending on non-renewable resources is not only are so many of them harmful to the larger ecosystem, but they also allow us to live so far beyond our means that when these resources begin to run out, we are left with a society that can no longer function properly. For example, can you imagine Los Angeles without the automobile or the American southwest as it currently exists without air conditioning? Our dependence on non-renewable resources has pushed our economic system beyond that which renewable systems can likely maintain.

An economic system based on renewable resources is not one in which growth for the sake of growth can be maintained, as resources need time to renew. Some, like bamboo, reach full maturity in 5 to 7 years, while a maple tree, by contrast takes 30 to 40 years to mature. A sustainable society cannot base itself on a business cycle driven by unchecked greed and excessive individualism, but rather needs to be tied into the rate at which its resources renew. As a lumberman, you wouldn't chop down trees faster then they renew because in the not too distant future you'd run out of trees and need to find another line of work. This is, in part, what happened to the residents of Easter Island as well as the romanticized disappearances of the Ansazi, early Mayan Society, and countless others. They consumed their resources faster than they could renew themselves, eventually causing their societies to collapse.

However, when most of those ancient societies collapsed, the people at least had the option of leaving and going elsewhere. Today, with an increasingly globally connected society, a population of several billion people, and an increasing number of environmentally degraded regions, there will not be enough places for all of us to run if an environmental collapse occurs. If we want to thrive as opposed to merely survive, we're going to have to find a way to transition our economic systems and our larger society. Herman Daly, the Emeritus Professor at the University of Maryland, School of Public Policy and former Chief Economist for the World Bank, who for more than two decades has tirelessly championed the need for alternative economic systems, suggests the following three rules for an ecologically sustainable economic system:

1. Renewable resources must be used no faster than the rate at which they regenerate.

2. Nonrenewable resources such as minerals and fossil fuels must be used no faster than renewable substitutes for them can be put into place.

3. Pollution and wastes must be emitted no faster than natural systems can absorb them, recycle them, or render them harmless.[26]

Our current global economic system not only does not allow for any of the behaviors Daly recommends, it actively inhibits those who act in accordance with these principles. After all, the sustainable lifestyle of the Kayapó peoples of Brazil is at risk not because they can't live within nature's limits, but rather because the rest of us can't.

If the central cause triggering our ecological problems is our economic system, the solution, then, should be to change that system. The entire field of environmental economics has emerged to tackle the problem that our economic system is not compatible with environment sustainability, with a number of perspectives emerging. For example, one school of thought suggests that the real problem is not growth, but rather that our economic system as is currently structured doesn't allow prices to fully reflect the environmental, as well as material and labor, costs of a product. For example, while the price of a cell phone includes the cost of mining the ore for the metals inside of it, drilling for oil for the plastic it contains, chopping down trees for its packaging, the energy consumed in assembling and shipping, and the labor costs, it does not include the loss of wildlife in that forest, the loss of the view of the forest, the money the government spends in rehabbing the mine, the loss in fresh drinking water, the money spent relocating an indigenous tribe off of their land to make the smelting of the materials in that cell phone possible, the high rate of birth defects among pregnant workers, the cost of increased rates of cancers amongst all workers in the plastic manufacturing facilities, and so on. If it did include the price of all of those things, what economists call negative externalities, a cell phone that cost $200 dollars might hypothetically cost $1,200. At that price, Americans would certainly be less inclined to purchase one, and we would definitely not upgrade every eighteen months, the current rate with which Americans currently toss out their cell phones for a new one.[28]

You can see the success of this kind of economic analysis as evidenced in the bag tax utilized by countries such as Ireland. Seeking to internalize (in the form of a tax) the cost to the environment (and to the country's sanitation department) of using bags, Ireland passed legislation requiring all stores to charge a thirty-cent per bag tax on all customers. While the tax was a success, removing some 1 billion bags from circulation, the problem with this kind of environmental accounting is it ignores the fact that we can't really account for every negative externality associated with every product. In addition, economic accounting of this nature does nothing to mitigate the system's need for us to buy more and more.

An alternative, and perhaps more intriguing theory put forth by Herman Daly and others is that of a *steady state economy.* A steady state economy is an economy that aims for stable population and stable consumption of energy and materials at sustainable levels.[28] If a growth economy is one that is dependent on an increase in the scale of what flows through an economic system from extraction, manufacture, distribution, consumption, and waste—a pathway known as throughput—a steady state economy is one in which the system's throughput remains constant. Or, as Herman Daly puts it, a steady state economy is "an economy with constant stocks of people and artifacts maintained at some desired, sufficient level by low rates of maintenance throughput." Points out Carolyn Merchant of the University of California at Berkley's Department of Conservation Resource Studies in her book *Radical Ecology: The Search for a Livable World*,

> The throughput is the flow of matter and energy from nonhuman nature, through the human economy, and back to nature as pollution [and waste]. A steady-state economy would use the lowest possible levels of materials and energy in the production phrase and emit the least possible amount of pollution in the consumption phase. The total population and the total amount of capital and consumer goods would be constant. The economy could continue to develop but need not grow. Culture, knowledge, ethics, and quality of life would continue to grow. Only physical materials would be constant.[29]

To borrow from our earlier analogy, if an 18 year old who is 5 feet 10 inches and 155 pounds would at age 65 be 30 feet tall and weigh more than 700 pounds under a growth economic system, under a steady state economy at 65 he would still be 5 feet 8 inches and weigh about 155 pounds. This doesn't, however, mean that nothing within the system would change. In much the same way that DVD's replaced videocassettes, things within a steady state economy would also be in a constant state of change. Innovation would not cease—it would just happen in harmony with the planet's natural limits. As an economic system, a steady state economy is more resilient to change, as well as more able to thrive alongside other different economic systems (assuming they're not a growth economy). Because we wouldn't be in a state of perpetual growth, we wouldn't be pressured to consume our neighbor's resources.

There's a poignant passage in Charles Long's book *How to Survive Without a Salary* wherein his family, who had made a deliberate financial and ecological decision not to own a clothes dryer, ran into a dilemma one winter. Their clothes were taking so long to hang dry that they would often run out of clothes before the last wash was completely dry. The problem, it seemed, was how to speed up the drying process. Their solution was to put aside their ethics and purchase a dryer. They were pondering where to put the dryer and where best to place the electrical hookup when they recognized that they had misidentified the problem. It was not that their clothes were taking too long to dry, but rather that they were running out of clothes too quickly. The easier, significantly cheaper, and far lighter on the earth solution was to pick up a few extra outfits at the local thrift store.

There lies within this tale of personal consumption a larger allegory for our society. It was not too long ago in human history that the very real problem was a problem of not enough. There was not enough food, not enough water, not enough health care. The solution to these problems was to increase the amount of stuff available, and the measure for tracking that, Gross Domestic Product, the value of all final goods and services produced within a country within a given period, seemed a good enough metric. Developed in 1934 by the economist Simon Smith Kuznets, GDP, however, was never intended to be an indicator of well-being. In fact, Kuznets explicitly cautioned against its use in that capacity, stating when he unveiled the metric that "The welfare of a nation can scarcely be inferred from a measurement of national income."[30] Kuznets understood intuitively what many of us still fail to grasp—that knowing how much income a nation generates tells us nothing about how that income is allocated or on what that income is being spent. It tells us nothing of a nation's well-being. And yet collectively, culturally, we've hitched ourselves to the GDP bandwagon. Points out the film *The Economics of Happiness*, "It's as if every problem we can have can be increased by solving GDP—poverty, unemployment, environmental decline. Using GDP as a measure of societal progress is little short of madness, if there's an oil spill, GDP goes up, if the water is so polluted we have to buy bottled water GDP goes up, war, cancer, an-epidemic, GDP goes up." As Senator Robert Kennedy eloquently stated in a 1968 speech at the University of Kansas,

> Gross National Product counts air pollution and cigarette advertising and the destruction of the redwood and the loss of our natural wonder in chaotic sprawl. It does not allow for the health of our children, the quality of their education or the joy of their play...the beauty of our poetry or the strength of our marriages. It measures everything, in short, except that which makes life worthwhile.[31]

It seems that what GDP has been allowing us to do is merely purchase a more expensive form of misery. True wellbeing is a mix of several things, including time spent in nature (a phenomena known as biophila), and, perhaps most importantly, relationships. A good chunk of what makes us happy, what makes us well, are relationships. Writes Robert Putnam in his book *Bowling Alone*

> Americans are right that the bonds of our communities have withered, and we are right to fear that this transformation has very real costs...most Americans today feel vaguely and uncomfortably disconnected...civic connections help make us healthy, wealthy, and wise....states whose residents trust other people, join organizations, volunteer, vote and socialize with friends - are the same states where children flourish: where babies are born healthy and where teenagers tend not to become parents, drop out of school, get involved in violent crime, or die prematurely due to suicide or homicide.[32]

The growth economy with its focus on more tends to weaken

the very things that we need to survive on an emotional level. According to the International Labour Organization, Americans work 137 more hours per year than Japanese workers, 260 more hours per year than British workers, and 499 more hours per year than French workers, which leaves us less time for family, for friends, for charity. Points out Yvon Chouinard, the founder of the clothing company Patagonia,

> Many of us in the United States live in what is thought to be abundance, with plenty all around us, but it is only an illusion, not the real thing. The economy we live in is marked by 'not enough.' We once asked the owner of a successful business if he had enough money and he replied, 'Don't you understand? There is never enough.' We don't have enough money, and we also don't have enough time. We don't have enough energy, solitude or peace...As Eric Hoffer, a mid-20th century philosopher, put it, 'You can never get enough of what you don't really need to make you happy.'[34]

According to the Happy Planet Index, a publication of the independent think-and-do tank The New Economics Foundation, the happiest country in the world is not the United States but rather Costa Rica, which manages to have the second-highest life expectancy in the West (behind Canada) along with the highest life satisfaction while using only a fraction of the natural resources of the US. Costa Rica has a footprint of 2.3 global hectares (an ideal footprint according to NEF would be 2.1). The United States ranks a pathetic 114th (out of 143 countries) with a footprint of 9.4, roughly four times larger than that of Costa Rica.[34] Even worse, our HPI or Happy Planet Index was higher thirty years ago (when we had less stuff but more time and better social relationships) than it is today.

Using the metrics that matter, we're clearly heading in the

wrong direction. The question then is how do we change course? Brian Czech, president of the nonprofit organization Center for the Advancement of the Steady State Economy, says that "There is a fundamental conflict between economic growth and environmental protection, economic sustainability, national security and international stability."

The question that remains is how do we resolve this conflict?

12. THE HAPPINESS ECONOMY

Environmentalism is not a spectator sport. People actually need to be vigilant about helping us maintain our clean air and water. —Lisa P. Jackson

What should young people do with their lives today? Many things, obviously. But the most daring thing is to create stable communities in which the terrible disease of loneliness can be cured.—Kurt Vonnegut, Jr.

Nestled high in the eastern Himalayas, with Chinese occupied Tibet to its north and India to its south, lays the Land of the Thunder Dragon, better known as the Kingdom of Bhutan. This tiny, isolated nation of some 700,000 people is home to the Gangkhar, a towering snow capped mountain that, at 22,623 feet, remains the world's largest unclimbed mountain peak (climbers are forbidden, lest they disturb the spirits). Covered by more than 60 percent virgin forest, Bhutan includes one of only 18 worldwide biodiversity hotspots, or regions with a significant amount of biodiversity that are at potential risk from human encroachment.[1] It also is the birthplace of Gross National Happiness.

First coined in 1972 by Bhutan's then King Jigme Singye Wangchuck, Gross National Happiness (GNH) is grounded in the recognition that wealth does not always lead to contentment. Unlike gross domestic product, which places economic growth squarely in the center of any discussion of human well-being, Bhutan's principle of Gross National Happiness takes a far more holistic approach, maintaining that economic growth by itself does not lead to human well-being. Instead of focusing exclusively on economic growth, GNH suggests that we focus instead on four pillars: economic self-reliance, a pristine environment, the preservation and promotion of culture, and good governance.[2]

What does this have to do with the environment? We started this journey with one simple question. Can we buy our way to a greener, more sustainable, planet? The evidence, from the heavy environmental toll that cars place on the planet regardless of their fuel source, to the ever-increasing consumptive demands of fashion, to the limits of our energy supply, suggests that we can't. Simply put, the scale and pace of our consumption cannot be supported through sustainable methods. To live within our planet's ecological limits, we are going to have to find a way to consume less, both of sustainable and non-sustainable resources.

While our economic system depends on us consuming more, the environment demands that we use less. This creates an uncomfortable tension between people and planet, of our short term well-being against our long term survival. If we continue our current pace of consumption, we will get to keep our creature comforts—for awhile. In the very near future, however, those comforts will be lost as we run out of resources. It's that simple. For some of the world's people, the clock has already run out, as they're already being confronted with the effects of resource destruction.

While we can't change the planets ecological limits, we can change our economy. King Wangchuck's proscription that public policy should be directly related to human well-being, to how people feel about their lives and not merely based on economic growth, may not only spell a way out of this tension between economic growth and environmental sustainability, but is also strongly in line with what we already know from the social sciences. Take for example this idea that money doesn't buy happiness. In economics, this concept is known as the Easterlin

Paradox, based on a 1974 study by economist Richard Easterlin, which pointed out that once you get past absolute levels of poverty, money doesn't automatically lead to increased levels of personal satisfaction.[3] This is likely why Americans today are no happier than they were three decades ago. During the post World War II era, the middle class grew, lifting millions out of poverty. Once that class was established, however, and people had left their previous levels of poverty behind, the effect of additional economic growth did nothing to increase their collective happiness.[4]

Overall, the idea of Gross National Happiness is both romantically appealing and inexplicably off-putting. On one hand, it appeals to our sense of having lost something very real, yet intangible, but of vital importance. When health experts have to create public service announcements because children are experiencing a resurgence of rickets because most of us can't seem to find the time, energy or wherewithal because of the demands of our economy to simply step outside our home and get enough sunlight to generate vitamin D, we've lost something.[5] When we work so many hours that we barely know our family members, never mind our neighbors, we've lost something. When our concept of a community extends more readily to the characters on our TV set than to our neighbor down the road, we've lost something.[6] And it isn't something that money can help us find.

The naturalist John Muir once wrote, "When we try to pick out anything by itself, we find it hitched to everything else in the universe."[7] We have tugged on the string of our ecological crisis and we found ourselves staring at our economy. It is an economic system that has rapidly become a lens that distorts how we see the world. So much of our culture has been framed and bent and mutated for a single purpose—to keep our economic engine churning. This thing, this idea that we created to serve humanity has increasingly become a thing that we humans serve, at the cost of our humanity. From a certain perspective, it might seem that what's happening to the earth may be the planet's desperate bid to get us to pay attention and fix things before it's too late.

This is not to say that Bhutan with its gross national happiness is perfect. It is still, in the ways that matter, a very poor country, with relatively high rates of infant mortality and issues of water quality and sanitation. Tensions exist between the Drukpas and the ethnic Nepalese who have been living in Southern Bhutan for decades. But in the handful of decades in which Bhutan has made the decision to join the outside world, they've made amazing strides in well-being while holding true to their core values. It is a nation that has actually improved its environment—Bhutan's forest cover is actually *increasing*. It is a country where the majority is content. As Tshewang Dendup, a graduate student at Berkeley who returned home to Bhutan after his studies, told Orville Schell, the dean of Berkeley's Graduate School of Journalism,

> The real appeal of Bhutan is that we feel human. Maybe we are somewhat isolated from the world, but we feel part of a living community that is not just connected by wires. That's why 95 percent of us exchange students return home. By and large, you would have to say people are happy here.[8]

How many Americans can say the same? How many of us are depressed? Anxious? Hyperactive? Or simply listless? We've been taught to believe that these diseases are biological. On the more extreme ends, this may be true. But compelling evidence suggests that on the more moderate and mild versions of the spectrum environment plays a huge role in our well-being and happiness. In Japan, they've found that a stroll through the forest fortifies not only the spirit but also the body, lowering blood pressure and normalizing blood sugars. Although the average American says that they believe nature is sacred or spiritual, we still spend 90 percent of our time indoors. Ultimately, our values and lives are mismatched and it's making many of us unhappy, even as it significantly harms the planet. Wouldn't it be nice to build an economic system based on the things that bring about both brief joy and lasting contentment, instead of on a growth paradigm that increasingly does neither? Wouldn't it be far more intelligent to create an economic system that is in harmony with our larger values of equality, of community, and yes of environmental protection, than to allow economic growth to ramrod over everything we hold near and dear? As activist Derrick Jensen argues,

> Does anyone really believe that Weyerhaeuser is going to stop deforesting because we ask nicely? Does anyone really believe that Monsanto will stop Monsantoing because we ask nicely? If only we get a Democrat in the White House, things will be okay. If only we pass this or that piece of legislation, things will be okay. If only we defeat this or that piece of legislation, things will be okay. Nonsense. Things will not be okay. They are already not okay, and they're getting worse. Rapidly.[9]

As Jensen says, we have to act now. However, individual action is not going to cut it. Instead, we need to get together. We need to organize. We need to collectivize. Vindana Shiva, in the film *The Economics of Happiness* says, "The only people who are deeply happy are people who know that they can depend on other people—lonely people have never been happy people."[10] So make yourself less lonely. Get to know your neighbors, start talking to your friends. Really start talking. Talk about your money problems, about your health, about your fears for the future. It's scary, but once you start talking to people a weird thing happens. You start to notice that all of the platitudes are true. We have more commonalities than differences. But even when we have differences, something else happens when the guy down the road stops being a stranger and starts being that fella who won't recycle. You know him. You know how to work with him, which makes the next step much, much, easier.

Once we get together, the next step is to start dropping out of the normal economic system. This isn't about becoming a freegan, or living simply—those are still individual actions that are dependent on the system as it currently stands. You couldn't be a freegan if our system didn't generate a tremendous amount of waste. What I'm talking about runs far deeper. It's about going to your neighborhood bars and getting them to band together to refuse to stock any beer sold by a publicly traded company, or getting your local bakeries to start using sustainably sourced flour, or getting people in your communities to stop frequenting the Wal-Mart's and big box retailers and to work together to localize the economy. It's about creating a *shadow*, or parallel, economy. Normally, when we hear about a shadow economy, we think about the drug trade, or nannies getting paid under table—economic actions that aren't captured by the "real" economy (the same "real" economy that is harming the environment). Typically, a shadow economy has negative connotations—often with good reason. The economy we're going to create, however, is about sustainability and community, so we can call it a light economy, because our economy will cast a light into the dark corners of the normal economy. It will tread lightly on the earth.

There are many ways of creating a light economy. Lots of people have already dabbled with it. In Ithaca, New York, they've created "Ithaca Hours," a form of legal currency that works to maintain the local economy by keeping money local, while in Japan, the government has sponsored several local level "community currency" programs designed to create social capital.[11] Transition Town initiatives, a global network of people working to build communities that are resilient enough to withstand the coming energy, climate and economic shocks while building a better quality of life in the process, have arisen from Asheville, North Carolina to Austin, Texas, from Ireland to Denmark, Latvia to South Africa and a myriad of places in between.[12]

Along the same lines, movements such as Slow Food, which "links the pleasure of food with a commitment to community and the environment," Slow Money, a national network committed to "new ways of thinking about the relationship between food, money and the environment" and Community Supported Agriculture, a community-based model of agriculture financing and food distribution, are all examples of people trying to build alternative economic models alongside our current economic system.[13] However, more of us need to either join in these efforts or start our own. We have to stop hoping others will lead us out of this mess, and start leading the way ourselves. For the people currently in power—some good, some bad, some indifferent—the systems as it stands works just fine. Thus, they have a vested interest in keeping things more or less the same. Changing the way our economy works doesn't mean ignoring existing political structures, though; the answer is not top down, or bottom up—it's both. But it must come from us.

Whatever we choose to do, there are some guiding principles we must follow, lest we be doomed to make the same mistakes and continue to spin in circles like a dog perennially chasing its tail. The first principle is that whatever system of living we chose to follow it **must be able to peacefully coexist with other, different, economic systems**. Under our current system, everyone must exist within the growth economy, or else the system will collapse. Historically, this was the source of tension between the American colonialists and the Native Americans, who had a lifestyle that was economically incompatible with that of the new settlers. When the indigenous population could not be converted, the next logical step under the growth paradigm was to eliminate them—and so we did, by deliberately and carefully exterminating the thing they were dependent on, the buffalo. Writes John Fire Lame Deer, an ineconju-Lakota Sioux born on the Rosebud Indian Reservation in South Dakota,

> The buffalo gave us everything we needed. Without it we were nothing. Our tipis were made of his skin. His hide was our bed, our blanket, our winter coat. It was our drum, throbbing through the night, alive, holy. Out of his skin we made our water bags. His flesh strengthened us, became flesh of our flesh. Not the smallest part of it was wasted. His stomach, a red-hot stone dropped into it, became our soup kettle. His horns were our spoons, the bones our knives, our women's awls and needles. Out of his sinews we made our bowstrings and thread. His ribs were fashioned into sleds for our children, his hoofs became rattles. His mighty skull, with the pipe leaning against it, was our sacred altar. The name of the greatest of all Sioux was Tatanka Iyotake—Sitting Bull. When you killed off the buffalo you also killed the Indian—the real, natural, "wild" Indian.[14]

The way we dealt with the Native American was to give him no other way of life but our own. So we undertook deliberate action to exterminate the buffalo, killing more buffalos in the 1870s than any other decade on record. As General Phil Sheridan explained in a speech regarding buffalo hunting delivered to the Texas Legislature in 1875:

> These men have done more in the last two years, and will do more in the next year, to settle the vexed Indian question, than the entire regular army has done in the last forty years. They are destroying the Indians' commissary. And it is a well known fact that an army losing its base of supplies is placed at a great disadvantage. Send them powder and lead, if you will; but for a lasting peace, let them kill, skin, and sell until the buffaloes are exterminated. Then your prairies can be covered with speckled cattle.[15]

That this genocide was necessary for our economic system is implicit in the way we tell America's creation story, in which the extermination of a people and their ways of being is viewed as a regrettable but necessary step in our evolution to the far more preferable present society. These days, this genocide continues at a rapid pace as culture after culture falls alternatively at the hands of business or at the end of a rifle to the economic reality of our inability to live within our own limits. Any economic system that cannot live peaceably with its neighbors, or that is predicated on its neighbors becoming more like it, is neither stable nor sustainable, and certainly not one that we should pursue or continue.

The next principle is that our **future systems must be nature-based**. The divorce from natural systems is what allows us to exist beyond our planetary limits. As Herman Daly writes,

> Economists have traditionally considered nature to be infinite relative to the economy, and therefore not scarce, and therefore properly priced at zero. But the biosphere is now scarce and becoming more so every day as a result of growth of its large and dependent subsystem, the macro-economy.[16]

This separation from nature isn't just bad for the environment; it's also bad for us. The growing field of biophilia, or humanity's innate need for nature, suggests that in separating humans from nature, we harm both. The traditional focus on minimizing humanity's ecological footprint misses the larger picture—humans need nature, and not merely as a resource base. Existing in spaces devoid of nature makes us more aggressive, depressive, slows cognitive function, increases hyperactivity and reduces self discipline.[17] In contrast, nature feeds and renews us. Hospital patients with views of green spaces heal faster than patients with a view of a wall or no window at all. The Japanese practice of Shinrin-yoku, loosely translated into "taking in the forest atmosphere" or "forest breathing" has been found to reduce blood sugar levels in diabetics, reduce the presence of stress markers such as cortisol, decrease blood pressure and increase the amount of cancer fighting enzymes present in our bodies.[18] Ecologist Joan Maloof writes in her book *Teaching the Trees* that "Researchers working in the Sierra Nevada of California found 120 chemical compounds in the mountain forest air, but they could identify only 70 of them! We are literally breathing things we don't understand. And when we lose our forests we don't know what we are losing."[19] The only way to hold onto nature is to value and celebrate it.

Finally, whatever we develop must be **locally-based**. This doesn't preclude global trade—I for one would think this life distinctly unpleasant if it meant I could never eat another mango—but it does mean that communities shouldn't have to depend on trade for their survival. When structures get too big, when the decisions for daily life become directed by people in very distant places who may have personal goals that lie in direct opposition of those they govern, problems arise. The former US Supreme Court Justice Louis Brandeis once said that "sunlight was the best disinfectant" reflecting the truth that in a transparent system, it's difficult for corruption to survive. Our current system is anything but transparent. A line in the film *The Economics of Happiness* states that "globalization is like having very long arms. So long that we aren't able to see what they are doing."[20] Localization allows for greater transparency. It also holds us as individuals accountable. Right now, it's too easy to shrug our shoulders and say that the problems are too large, the people too powerful, the situation too far outside of our control. These are all positions that are far less simple to take when the structures in question are in our own backyards.

This book began by taking a critical look at the products, systems and structures that we are repeatedly told will help us to usher in a sustainable future. Many of us desperately want to believe that we can shop our way to sustainability. We like this idea because it's comfortable to think that we can go on living the way we are currently living, and that structures put into place centuries ago can carry us into an ever improving future. However, most of these "green" products crumbled under the light of the barest scrutiny, and the evidence shows that the past can no longer be a template for our future.

Faced with the reality that we have to change, we take comfort in the notion that someone or something—the right politician, the right corporation, the right philanthropist, the right technology, the right product—will come along and fix everything. Yet as Parisian street graffiti from the nation's civil unrest in 1968 cautions, "vous finirez tous par crever du confort," which translates to "you will end up dying of comfort." There was already an awareness forty years ago that taking the comfortable route is no different than covering our ears and closing our eyes and pretending that we can't see the oncoming freight train. This attitude won't stop us, however, from being run over. The braver, more exciting thing to do is to open our eyes, uncap our ears and walk with our senses open, fully aware, into the future, trying with every step to make things better. What could be more fun than working together to improve our world?

ACKNOWLEDGEMENTS

Writing this book has been one of the most challenging, exciting, frustrating, hopeful, scary, wonderful things I have ever done. I wouldn't have made it through without the emotional and grammatical support of so many people. Thank you to Allison, Esra, Debbie, Jarret, Elina, Brenda, Renae, Susan and Jaeah for being constant sources of support and reassurance throughout this process. Cristina for making me smile when I wanted to sigh, Steve V for serving as a reminder of what I was working towards, Steve R for reading far too many excerpts over a questionable internet connection, Dave for his constant source of wisdom, Lucie, John, JY and Justin for being constant sources of (admittedly welcomed) procrastination, Kate for lending me her ear to bounce my ideas off of, my parents and my editor, Robert, for putting up with me, and Idelle for her willingness to do some of my grunt work. If I've left anyone out, I'm so sorry, but really thank you!

NOTES

INTRODUCTION: EMPTO ERGO SUM

1. Convention on Biological Diversity, Sustaining Life on Earth, April 2000, http://www.cbd.int/convention/guide.shtml?id=action

2. David R. Boyd, "Prescription for a Healthy Canada: Towards A National Environmental Health Strategy," (David Suzuki Foundation, Vancouver, September 2007),http://www.davidsuzuki.org/publications/downloads/2007/DSF-Prescription-for-Canada-Full-Research.pdf

3. Boyd, "Prescription for a Healthy Canada."

4. Philippe Duboc, Hassan Hajjaj, and Peter Niederberger, "Lovastatin Biosynthesis by Aspergillus terreus in a Chemically Defined Medium," *Applied and Environmental Microbiology* 67, (June 2001): 2596-2602.

5. Mintel Oxygen Reports, "Mintel finds fewer Americans interested in going "green" during recession," United States, 2009.

6. Robert Putnam, *Bowling Alone*, (New York: Simon & Schuster, 2001).

1.GREEN IS THE NEW BLACK

1. Anna Kuchment, "Sense and Sensibility," *Newsweek*, April 5, 2008.

2. Nathaniel Dafydd Beard, "The Branding of Ethical Fashion and the consumer: A Luxury Niche or Mass-market Reality?," *Fashion Theory*, 2008: 447-468.

3. Packaged Facts, "International Market for Sustainable (Green) Apparel," Market Research Group, LLC, Rockville, MD, 2008.

4. Kate Eshelby, "Organic Cotton," *Ecologist,* February 2006: 34-39

5. A.K. Chapagain, A.Y. Hoekstra, H.H.G. Savenije, and R. Gautam, "The water footprint of cotton consumption," Value of Water Research Report Series, no.18 (2005), UNESCO-IHE.

6. Environmental Justice Foundation, "The Aral Sea Crisis", http://

www.ejfoundation.org/page146.html

7. Ibid.

8. William Neuman, "Amber Waves to Ivory Bolls, *New York Times*, March 28, 2011, http://www.nytimes.com/2011/03/29/business/29cotton.html

9. Louise R. Morgan and Grete Birtwistle, "An Investigation of Young Fashion Consumer's Disposal Habits," *International Journal of Consumer Studies*, 2009: 190-198.

10. (Surface Design 2009)

11. (Sustainable Development 2010)

12. Wendy Tremayne, Swap-O-Rama-Rama, http://swaporama-rama.org/

2: HOW WE EAT

1. USDA Natural Resources Conservation Service, "Effects of Conservation Practices on Cultivated Cropland in the Upper Mississippi River Basin Government Report," 2010.

2. Jonathan Watts, "Exploding watermelons put spotlight on Chinese farming practices," *The Guardian,* May 17, 2011.

3. Q Hu, WJ Nelson, ET Spiliotis, "Forchlorfenuron alters mammalian septin assembly, organization, and dynamics," *The Journal of Biological Chemistry,* October 24, 2008: 63-71.

4. Lauren Etter, "Manure Raises New Stink," *The Wall Street Journal*, March 25, 2010.

5. Marcel Aillery, "United States Department of Agriculture Economic Research Service: Irrigation and Water Use," United States Department of Agriculture, November 22, 2004, http://www.ers.usda.gov/Briefing/WaterUse/

6. Jane Braxton Little, "The Ogallala Aquifer: Saving a Vital U.S. Water Source," *Scientific American* 30, March 2009.

7. Charles Laurence, "US farmers fear the return of the Dust Bowl,"The Telegraph, March 7, 2011.

8. Little, "The Ogallala Aquifer."

9. Little, "The Ogallala Aquifer."

10. Dave Thier, "Time, Water Running Out for America's Biggest Aquifer,"AOL News, April 20, 2010.

11. Little, "The Ogallala Aquifer."

12. Charles Laurence, "US farmers fear the return of the Dust Bowl," *The Telegraph*, March 7, 2011.

13. William Ashworth, *Ogallala Blue: Water and Life on the High Plains* (New York: W.W. Norton, 2007).

14. Food & Water Watch, "Unmeasured Danger: America's Hidden Groundwater Crisis," fact sheet (Washington DC, 2009), http://documents.foodandwaterwatch.org/groundwater.pdf.

15. Save the Colorado River 2010, http://www.savethecolorado.org/river.php.

16. Leo Horrigan, Leo, Robert S. Lawrence, and Polly Walker, "How Sustainable Agriculture Can Address the Environmental and Human Health Harms of Industrial Agriculture," *Environmental Health Perspectives* 110, no. 5 (2002): 445-446.

17. U.S. Environmental Protection Agency, "Inventory of U.S. Greenhouse Gas Emissions and Sinks: 1990-2009," 2011 U.S. Greenhouse Gas Inventory Report..

18. John Vidal, "Why is the Gates foundation investing in GM giant Monsanto?" *The Guardian*, September 29, 2010.

19. Tom Philpot, "Bill Gates reveals support for GMO ag," Grist.org, October 21, 2009, http://www.grist.org/article/2009-10-21-bill-gates-reveals-support-for-gmo-ag.

20. National Agricultural Statistics Service, Agricultural Statistics Board, USDA, "Acreage Report," June 30, 2011.

21. William Neuman and Andrew Pollack, "Rise of the Superweeds," *New York Times*, May 4, 2010.

22. Philip Brasher, "Roundup-resistant weeds are cropping up," *Des Moines Register*, 2003.

23. Joshua Davis, "The Mystery of the Coca Plant That Wouldn't Die," *Wired*, November 2004.

24. Cormac Sheridan, "Report blames GM crops for herbicide spike, downplays pesticide reductions," *Nature Biotechnology*, February 2010: 112-113.

25. Charles Benbrook, "Impacts of Genetically Engineered Crops on Pesticide Use: The First Thirteen Years," The Organic Center, 2009.

26. Neuman and Pollack, "Rise of the Superweeds."

27. IFOAM (International Federation of Organic Agriculture Movements), "Definition of Organic Agriculture," 2009, http://www.ifoam.org/growing_organic/definitions/doa/index.html

28. Denis Lairon, "Nutritional quality and safety of organic food. A review," *Agronomy for Sustainable Development*, January 2010: 33-41.

29. P Baker, Brian, Charles M. Benbrook, Edward Growth III, and Karen Lutz Benbrook., "Pesticide residues in conventional, IPM-grown

and organic foods: Insights from three U.S. data sets," *Food Additives and Contaminants* 19, no.5 (May 2002).

30. Chensheng Lu, Kathryn Toepel, Rene Irish, Richard A. Fenske, Dana B. Barr, and Roberto Bravo, "Organic Diets Significantly Lower Children's Dietary Exposure to Organophosphorus Pesticides," *Environmental Health Perspectives*, February 2006: 260-263.

31. John P Reganold, et al, "Fruit and Soil Quality of Organic and Conventional Strawberry Agroecosystems," *PLoS ONE* , September 1, 2010.

32. National Cancer Institute at NIH, "Agricultural Health Study," fact sheet, June 16, 2011, http://www.cancer.gov/cancertopics/factsheet/Risk/ahs

33. Ibid.

34. Michelle A Mendez, et al, "Prenatal Organochlorine Compound Exposure, Rapid Weight Gain, and Overweight in Infancy," *Environmental Health Perspectives*, October 5, 2010: 272-278.

35. Verhulst, Stijn L., et al, "Intrauterine Exposure to Environmental Pollutants and Body Mass Index during the First 3 Years of Life," *Environmental Health Perspectives*, October 8, 2008: 122-126.

36. Leon T. Lassiter and Stephen Brimijoin, "Rats gain excess weight after developmental exposure to the organophosphorothionate pesticide, chlorpyrifos," *Neurotoxicology and Teratology*, March-April 2008: 125-130.

37. Food and Agriculture Organization of the United Nations, "The State of Food Insecurity in the World 2010."

38. Ibid.

39. Olivier De Schutter, "Agroecology and the Right to Food," Report presented at the 16th Session of the United Nations Human Rights Council, March 2011.

40. United Nations, "Eco-Farming Can Double Food Production in 10 Years Says New UN Report," March 8, 2011. http://www.unog.ch/80256EDD006B9C2E/(httpNewsByYear_en)/9803052BF59C7EB5C125784D004CEE0F?OpenDocument

41. Union of Concerned Scientists, "Failure to Yield: Biotechnology's Broken Promises," 2009.

42. Rich Pirog and Andrew Benjamin, "Checking the Food Odometer: Comparing Food Miles for Local Versus Conventional Produce Sales in Iowa Institution," Leopold Center for Sustainable Agriculture, 2003.

43. Earthbound Farm Organic, "About Earthbound," http://www.

ebfarm.com/AboutUs/index.aspx

44. Sharon Pian Chan, ""One giant step for goatkind: Seattle gives them pet status," *Seattle Times*, September 25, 2007.

45. Lufa Farms, "Combiner les produits frais des Fermes Lufa avec les produits de nos agriculteurs locaux," https://lufa.com/panier_local_petit_alternatif.

46. Christopher L. Weber, and H. Scott Matthews, "Food-Miles and the Relative Climate Impacts of Food Choices in the United States," *Environmental Science & Technology*, 2008: 3508–3513.

47. Choy Leng Yeong, "NW salmon sent to China before reaching U.S. tables," *Seattle Times*, July 16, 2005: http://seattletimes.nwsource.com/html/businesstechnology/2002384544_uschinafish16.html.

48. Brian Halweil, "Where Have All the Farmers Gone?" *World Watch Magazine*, 2000.

49.Eat, Move, Sleep Blog, "Quote from Carlo Petrini: Founder of Slow Food Movement," http://eatmovesleep.posterous.com/quote-from-carlo-petrini-founder-of-the-slow

50. US EPA., "Wastes - Resource Conservation - Common Wastes & Materials - Organic Materials - Food Waste," (accessed on December 16, 2010); "Wastes - Resource Conservation - Common Wastes & Materials - Organic Materials" (accessed December 30, 2010).

51. Kevin D. Hall, Juen Guo, Michael Dore, and Carson C. Chow,"The Progressive Increase of Food Waste in America and Its Environmental Impact," *PLoS ONE*, November 25, 2009.

52. Ibid.

53. Mark Nord, Alisha Coleman-Jensen, Margaret Andrews, and Steven Carlson, "Household Food Security in the United States, 2009," ERR-1018, US Department of Agriculture, Economic Research Service, November 2010.

54. Worldwatch Institute, *2011 State of the World: Innovations that Nourish the Planet* (Washington, DC: 2011).

55. Jenny Gustavsson, Christel Cederberg, Ulf Sonesson, Robert van Otterdijk, and Alexandre Meybeck, "Global Food Losses and Food waste Extent Causes and Prevention," Food and Agriculture Organization of the United Nations, 2011.

56. Nord, Coleman-Jensen, Andrews and Carlson, "Household Food Security in the United States."

57. CIA, "Country Comparison: Oil Consumption," CIA: The World Factbook 2009, https://www.cia.gov/library/publications/the-world-factbook/rankorder/2174rank.html (accessed 9 29, 2011).

58. U.S. Energy Information Administration:Office of Integrated Analysis and Forecasting, "Emissions of Greenhouse Gases in the United States 2008," government report, U.S. Department of Energy, 2009.

3: HOW GREEN IS CLEAN?

1. Mary Fischer, "Scared Straight," *Allure*, 2007.

2. Mike Brunker, "Are FEMA trailers 'toxic tin cans'?" *MSNBC*, July 25, 2006, http://www.msnbc.msn.com/id/14011193/ns/us_news-katrina_the_long road_back/t/are-fema-trailers-toxic-tin cans/ (accessed September 26, 2011).

3. Oregon OSHA and CROET at Oregon Health and Sciences University, "'Keratin-Based' Hair Smoothing Products And the Presence of Formaldehyde," research report, October 2010.

4. James Covert, "Brazilian Blowout sues OSHA in Oregon," *New York Post*, December 16, 2010.

5. A di Nardo, K Sugino, P Wertz, J Ademola, and HI Maibach, "Sodium lauryl sulfate (SLS) induced irritant contact dermatitis: a correlation study between ceramides and in vivo parameters of irritation," *Contact Dermatitis*, August 1996: 86-91.

6. PD Darbre and PW Harvey, "Paraben esters: review of recent studies of endocrine toxicity, absorption, esterase and human exposure, and discussion of potential human health risks," *Journal of Applied Toxicology*, July 2008: 561-578.

7. Ibid.

8. Yoshinori Okamoto, Tomohiro Hayashi, Shinpei Matsunami, Koji Ueda, and Nakao Kojima, "Combined Activation of Methyl Paraben by Light Irradiation and Esterase Metabolism toward Oxidative DNA Damage," *Chemical Research in Toxicology*, July 2008: 1594-1599.

9. Roberto Danovaro, et al, "Sunscreens Cause Coral Bleaching by Promoting Viral Infections," *Environmental Health Perspectives*, January 3, 2008: 441-447.

10. Lyndsey Layton, "FDA says studies on triclosan, used in sanitizers and soaps, raise concerns," *Washington Post*, April 8, 2010.

11. Environmental News Service, "Dioxin Poisoning Scars Ukrainian Presidential Candidate," December 13, 2004, http://www.ens-newswire.com/ens/dec2004/2004-12-13-03.html (accessed February 15, 2011).

12. Lyndsey Layton, "FDA says studies on triclosan, used in sanitizers

and soaps, raise concerns," *Washington Post*, April 8, 2010.

13. Jane Houlihan, "Why this matters – Cosmetics and your health," Environmental Working Group, Skin Deep Database, April 13, 2011.

14. Ibid.

15. Center for Environmental Health, "Lawsuit Launched to End Mislabeling of "Organic" Personal Care Products," press release, June 2011.

16. *Time Magazine*, "Behind The Pretty Picture," February 27, 2007, http://www.time.com/time/magazine/article/0,9171,1594138-2,00.html

4: THE GREEN CAR MYTH: THINKING BEYOND THE TAIL PIPE

1. Eduardo Galeano, *Upside Down: A Primer for the Looking-Glass World* (New York: Picador, 2005).

2. Sarah Rose, "America's Most Scenic Roads: Hit the road and enjoy the scenic views from Hawaii to Rhode Island," *Travel+Leisure*, April 2011.

3. James Howard Kuntsler, *The Geography of Nowhere: The Rise and Decline of America's Man-Made Landscape* (New York: Free Press, 1994).

4. John M. Gibbons, "I Can't Get No...Job Satisfaction, That Is," survey byThe Conference Board, January 2010.

5. US Department of Labor and US Bureau of Labor Statistics, "Consumer Expenditures in 2009," Report 1029, 2011.

6. Brian McKenzie, Melanie Rapino, et, "American Community Surveys: Commuting in the United States: 2009," government report, US Census Bureau, 2011.

7. US Department of Transportation, Federal Highway Administration, "Highway Statistics 2009: Licensed Drivers, Vehicle Registrations, and Resident Population," 2011.

8. Shohln Freeman, "Pollution in Overdrive," *Washington Post*, June 28, 2006.

9. US Department of Transportation, "Highway Statistics 2009."

10. Bill McKibben, "When Words Fail," *Orion Magazine*, July/August 2008.

11. (Office of Energy Efficiency and Renewable Energy; US EPA 2010)

12. US Department of Energy, "Carbon Sequestration," http://www.energy.gov/sciencetech/carbonsequestration.htm (accessed January 10, 2011).

13. Vicki Haddock, "Oh, so pious, Prius drivers / Smugness drifts over the warming Earth -- is that a bad thing?" *San Francisco Chronicle*, July 15, 2007.

14. Steven E. Sexton and Alison L. Sexton, "Conspicuous Conservation: The Prius Effect and Willingness to Pay for Environmental Bona Fides," working paper, American Economic Association, 2010.

15. Toyota Motor Sales, "Toyota Sells One-Millionth Prius in the U.S." press release, Los Angeles, CA, 2011.

16. René Diekstra and Martin Kroon, "Cars and Behaviour: Psychological Barriers to Car Restraint and Sustainable Urban Transport," in *The Greening of Urban Transport*, ed. Rodney S Tolley, (Jersey City: Wiley, 1997), 147-161

17. Research and Innovative Technology Administration (RITA) and Department of Transportation, "Table 4-9: Motor Vehicle Fuel Consumption and Travel," 2010, http://www.bts.gov/publications/national_transportation_statistics/html/table_04_09.html (accès le October 4, 2011).

18. Jonathan W. Fox and David R. Cramer, "Hypercars: A Market-Oriented Approach to Meeting Lifecycle Environmental Goals," Society of Automotive Engineers, Rocky Mountain Institute, CO, 1997.

19. Chuck Squatriglia, "Go Green — Buy a Used Car. It's Better Than a Hybrid," *Wired*, May 19, 2008.

20. Matt Powers, "Don't Buy That New Prius! Test-Drive a Used Car Instead," *Wired*, May 19, 2008.

21. Vicki Haddock, "Oh, so pious, Prius drivers / Smugness drifts over the warming Earth—is that a bad thing?" *San Francisco Chronicle*, July 15, 2007.

22. Stephen T. Muench, "Roadway Construction Sustainability Impacts Review of Life-Cycle Assessments," *Transportation Research Record: Journal of the Transportation Research Board*, September 22, 2010: 36-45.

23. Guangqing Chi and Brian Stone, Jr., "Sustainable Transport Planning: Estimating the Ecological Footprint of Vehicle Travel in Future Year," *Journal of Urban Planning and Develpment*, September 2005: 170-180.

24. (Research and Innovative Technology Administration Bureau of Transportation Statistics 2009)

25. Brenner, Elsa. "Matching a Dream to a Budget," *New York Times*, October 16, 2005.

26. Michelle Conlin,"Extreme Commuting," *Businessweek*, February

21, 2005.

27. Erin Anderssen, "Stuck with a long commute? Your marriage may be at risk," *The Globe and Mail-Blog*, May 25, 2011, . http://www.theglobeandmail.com/life/the-hot-button/stuck-with-a-long-commute-your-marriage-may-be-at-risk/article2036226/ (accessed October 4, 2011).

28. Gilbert N. Hanson, "Bicycling in Muenster, Germany," State University of New York at Stony Brook Department of Geosciences. http://www.geo.sunysb.edu/bicycle-muenster/index.html (accessed on October 4, 2011).

29. Lawyer, David S. "Bicycle Energy." Bicycle Energy. February 2008. http://www.lafn.org/~dave/trans/energy/bicycle-energy.html (accès le October 3, 2011).

5: HOW CLEAN IS YOUR CANTEEN?

1. Pacific Institute, "Bottled Water and Energy: Getting to 17 Million Barrels," fact sheet, Oakland, CA, 2007.

2. New York State Department of Environmental Conservation, "Too Many Bottles—It's a Waste," fact sheet, Albany, NY.

3. Susan Casey, "Garbage In, Garbage Out," *Conservation Magazine*, January-March 2010.

4. Anish Kelkar, Richard Roth, and Joel Clark, "Automobile Bodies: Can Aluminum Be an Economical Alternative to Steel?" *Journal of the Minerals, Metals and Materials Society* 53, no. 8 (August 2001): 28-32.

5. International Aluminium Institute, "Fourth Sustainable Bauxite Mining Report: IV 2008," annual report, 2009.

6. U.S. Environmental Protection Agency, "ALCOA, Inc.: Clean Air Act Civil Judicial Settlement," http://www.epa.gov/compliance/resources/cases/civil/caa/alcoa.html (accessed on October 4, 2011).

7. Daniel Martineau, et al., "Cancer in Wildlife, a Case Study: Beluga from the St. Lawrence Estuary, Quebec, Canada," *Environmental Health Perspectives*, March 2002: 285-292.

8. John Nadler, "Hungary Continues to Battle Its Toxic Flood," *Time*, October 7, 2010.

9. Michael Smith and Adriana Brasileiro, "Alcoa Razes Rain Forest in Court Case Led by Brazil Prosecutors," *Bloomberg*, July 30, 2009.

10. Ibid.

11. Ylan Q. Mui, "Bottled Water Boom Appears Tapped Out," *Washington Post*, August 13, 2009.

12. International Bottled Water Association, "U.S. Bottled Water Volume Grew 3.5% in 2010 as Economic Conditions Begin to Improve," press release, 2011.

6: THE GREENEST BUILDING

1. Jay Shafer, "Philosophy: Dream Big. Build Small," Tumbleweed Tiny House Company, http://www.tumbleweedhouses.com/jay/ (accessed March 4, 20110.

2. Ibid.

3. US Bureau of the Census, *Census of Population: 1950 United States Summary-Volume I Part 1*, (Washington, DC: Government Printing Office, 1953).

4. US Bureau of the Census, "Median and Average Square Feet of Floor Area in New Single-Family Houses Completed by Location," http://www.census.gov/const/C25Ann/sftotalmedavgsqft.pdf (accessed October 19, 2011).

5. Ibid.

6. Chris Kraul, "Builders Cut Corners in Recession: Housing: Size, quality and cost of homes are being scaled down to boost sales in midst of a slump," *Los Angeles Times*, September 24, 1991.

7.US Census: Fertility and Family Statistics Branch. U.S. Census Bureau, Current Population Survey, March and Annual Social and Economic Supplements, 2010 and earlier. Washington, DC: November, 2010.

8. Matt Taibbi, "Flat N All That," *New York Press*, January 14, 2009.

9. Amy Rowland, "Smile When You Call Them McMansions," *New York Times*, June 5, 2005.

10. J.L. Nasar and J Evans-Cowley, "McMansions: The extent and regulations of super-sized Homes," *Journal of Urban Design* 12, no. 3: 339-358.

11. Les Christie, "Die, die, monster home! Die!" *CNN Money*, August 18, 2005.

12. Judith Helfand and Daniel B Gould, "The Lifecycle of Vinyl: Past, Present and Future Harm," Blue Vinyl, http://www.bluevinyl.org/PVC.pdf (accessed December 15, 2010).

13. WHO Health Organization,"Dioxins and their effects on human health," May 5, 2010, http://www.who.int/mediacentre/factsheets/fs225/en/ (accessed on December 14, 2010).

14. Les Stone, "Cancer Alley Louisiana," Witness, An online maga-

zine.

15. US Environmental Protection Agency, "Chromated Copper Arsenate (CCA): Consumer Safety Information Sheet: inorganic Arsenical Pressure-Treated Wood," fact sheet, (accessed on October 19, 2011).

16. Healthy Building Network, "Toxic Chemicals in Building Materials: An Overview for Health Care Organizations," fact sheet, May 2008.

17. Cole Sonafrank, "Substantially Superior Cements: An Introduction to Magnesium Phosphate Cements (MPCs) and Geopolymers," Cold Climate Research Center Snapshot, 2008.

18. US Green Building Council, "Building Impacts: Why Build Green?" Power Point presentation, 2009.

19. Office of the Federal Environmental Executive,"The Federal Commitment to Green Building: Experiences and Expectations," 2003.

20. US Green Building Council, "Rating Systems,"US Green Building Council, http://www.usgbc.org/DisplayPage.aspx?CMSPageID=222 (accessed on October 17, 2011).

21. *Philadelphia Inquirer*, "Green Building Advocates Take The LEED," April 11, 2010.

22. *Chicago Agent Magazine*, "Green Home Building Passes 10,000 LEED-certified Homes Milestone," April 7, 2011, http://chicagoagentmagazine.com/green-home-building-passes-10000-leed-certified-homes-milestone/ (accessed May 1, 2011).

23. Kelly Minner, "10,000 LEED-certified Homes," ArcDaily.April 14, 2011, http://www.archdaily.com/127657/10000-leed-certified-homes/ (accessed May 1, 2011).

24. "Case Study: The Go Green Home," Go Green Construction, http://www.gogreencalifornia.com/case.html (accessed May 3 2011, 2011).

25. Green Building Initiative, "Green Globes," http://www.thegbi.org/green-globes/ (accessed October 19, 2011).

26. Henry Gifford, "A Better Way to Rate Green Buildings," working paper, September 11, 2008, http://www.energysavingscience.com/articles.

27. Ibid.

28. Alex Wilson, "Rethinking the All-Glass Building," *Environmental Building News*, June 2010.

29. Lisa Prevost, "How 'Green' Can a Huge House Be?" *New York Times*, April 6, 2008.

30. Carl Elefante, "The Greenest Building Is...One That Is Already

Built," *Forum Journal* 21, no. 4 (2007): 26-38.

31. Wayne Curtis, "A Cautionary Tale: Amid our green-building boom, why neglecting the old in favor of the new just might cost us dearly," *Preservation*, January/February 2008.

32. Christopher B. Leinberger, "The Next Slum?," *Atlantic,* March 2008.

33. Ibid.

34. David Easton, *The Rammed Earth House: Rediscovering the Most Ancient Building Material* (White River Junction, Vermont: Chelsea Green Publishing Company, 1996).

35. Lester Boyer, "Earth Sheltered Structures," *Annual Review of Energy* 7 (November 1982): 201-219.

36. Sarah Susanka and Kira Obolensky, *The Not So Big House: A Blueprint for the Way We Really Live* (Newton, CT: Taunton Press, 2009).

7: THE CLEAN COAL MYTH

1. American Coalition for Clean Coal Electricity, "Clean Coal:60 TV Spot 'I Believe'," April 16,2008, http://www.youtube.com/user/balancedenergy#p/u/76/X_5OrJVR_Vc (accessed on November 7, 2011).

2. Ibid.

3. Kevin Krajick, "Fire in the Hole," *Smithsonian*, May 2005.

4. Weird US, "Centralia's Fire Down Below," http://www.weirdus.com/states/pennsylvania/abandoned/centralia/index.php (accessed November 7, 2011)

5. Krajick, "Fire in the Hole."

6. Allan Kolker et al., "Emissions from Coal Fires and Their Impact on the Environment," fact sheet 2009-3084, US Geological Survey.

7. Jane Macartney, "Coalmine fire put out after half a century," *The Times*, November 22, 2007.

8. Kolker, "Emissions from Coal Fires."

9. US Department of Energy, "Carbon Sequestration," http://www.energy.gov/sciencetech/carbonsequestration.htm (accessed January 10, 2011).

10. Carl Zimmer, "An Ominous Warning on the Effects of Ocean Acidification," *Yale Environment 360*, February 15, 2010.

11. Bert Metz, et al., *IPCC Special Report on Carbon Dioxide Capture and Storage* (New York: Cambridge University Press, 2005).

12. Stephanie Smith, "Months after ash spill, Tennessee town still

choking," July 13 2009, *CNN* http://articles.cnn.com/2009-07-13/health/coal.ash.illnesses_1_coal-ash-drinking-water-coal-power-plant/3?_s=PM:HEALTH (accessed on November 7, 2011).

13. Scott Barker, "The coal ash spill catastrophe in Kingston - One year later," *Knoxville News Sentinel*, December 19, 1998.

14. Smith, "Months after ash spill."

15. US Environmental Protection Agency, "2005 National Emissions Inventory Data & Documentation."

16. US Environmental Protection Agency, "Human and Ecological Risk Assessment of Coal Combustion Wastes," Draft, prepared by RTI International, August 2007.

17. U.S. Bureau of the Census, "Perry County Quickfacts from the US Census Bureau," http://quickfacts.census.gov/qfd/states/01/01105.html (accessed November 15, 2011).

18. Perry County. Dirs. N'Jeri Eaton and Matt Durning. Perf. N'Jeri Eaton and Matt Durning. 2010.

19. U.S. Congress Committee on Transportation and Infrastructure, Subcommittee on Water Resources and Environment of the Committee on Transportation and Infrastructure, *The One-Year Anniversary of the Tennessee Valley Authority's Kingston Ash Slide: Evaluating Current Cleanup Progress and Assessing Future Environmental Goals*, Hearing No. 111-19, 111th Congress, March 31, 2009.

20. Laura Basset, "Even The Cows Have Cancer: EPA Weighs Tougher Regulation of Toxic Coal Ash," March 24, 2010, *Huffington Post*, http://www.huffingtonpost.com/2010/03/24/even-the-cows-have-cancer_n_511214.html (accessed November 7, 2011).

21. Jonathan Hiskes, "You'll Be Sorry Ms. Jackson: Rural county asks EPA chief not to make it 'The Ash Hole of Alabama'," Grist, July 7, 2009.

22. Rob Perks, "Appalachian Heartbreak: Time to End Mountaintop Removal Coal Mining," issue paper, Natural Resources Defense Council, November 2009.

23. Ibid.

24. Michael Hendryx, Leah Wolfe, Juhua Luo and Bo Webb, "Self-Reported Cancer Rates in Two Rural Areas of West Virginia with and Without Mountaintop Coal Mining," *Journal of Community Health*, July 24, 2011.

8: THE BIOFUEL REVOLUTION

1. US Department of Energy, "How Fossil Fuels were Formed," Ocotber 9, 2008, http://fossil.energy.gov/education/energylessons/coal/gen_howformed.html

2. Caroline Henshaw, "Land for Biofuels or Crops? The Debate Rumbles on," *Wallstreet Journal* June 22, 2011.

3. Monte Reel, "Brazil's Road to Energy Independence," *Washington Post*, August 20, 2006.

4. Holly Jessen, "Open Fuel Standard Bill Progresses, but Slowly," *Ethanol Producer Magazine*, June 8, 2011.

5. Seth Borenstein, "Ethanol may cause more smog, more deaths," *Associated Press*, April 18, 2007.

6. Ibid.

7. Texas Comptroller of Public Account,"The Energy Report," 2008.

8. Hosein Shapouri, James A. Duffield and Michael Wang, "The Energy Balance of Corn Ethanol: An Update," US Department of Agriculture, 2002.

9. David Pimentel and Tad W. Patzek, "Ethanol Production Using Corn, Switchgrass, and Wood; Biodiesel Production Using Soybean and Sunflower," *Natural Resources Research* 14.1 (2005): 65-76.

10. Reel, "Brazil's Road to Energy Independence."

11. Christopher Matthews,"Deforestation causes global warming," September 4, 2006, Food and Agriculture Organization of the United Nations, http://www.fao.org/newsroom/en/news/2006/1000385/index.html (accessed October 9, 2010).

12. Simon L. Lewis, "The 2010 Amazon Drought," *Science* 331, no. 6017 (2011): 554.

13. Stuart Grudgings, "Amazon drought caused huge carbon emissions -study," *Reuters*, February 3, 2011.

14. David Biello, "Peat and Repeat: Can Major Carbon Sinks Be Restored by Rewetting the World's Drained Bogs?" *Scientific American* December 8, 2009.

15. Lian Pin Koh, et al., "Remotely sensed evidence of tropical peatland conversion to oil palm," Proceedings of the National Academy of Sciences, March 2, 2011.

16. David Suzuki and Faisal Moola, "Biofuels not necessarily all that green," Science Matters blog, September 14, 2007, http://www.davidsuzuki.org/blogs/science-matters/2007/09/biofuels-not-necessarily-all-that-green/ (accessed January 15, 2011)

17. Bryan Walsh, "Tropicana: Trying to Make a Greener Orange Juice," *Time*, March 11, 2010.

18. University of Iowa: Center for Health Effects of Environmental Contamination, "Iowa Statewide Rural Well Water Survey Phase 2 (SWRL2) : Results and Analysis," August 2009.

19. World Health Organization, "Water-related diseases: Methaemoglobinemia," fact sheet, 2001.

20. PJ Weyer, et al., "Municipal drinking water nitrate level and cancer risk in older women: the Iowa Women's Health Study." *Epidemiology*, May 2001: 327-338.

21. Pimentel and Patzek, "Ethanol Production Using Corn."

22. ActionAid International, "Cereal Offenders?: How the G8 has Contributed to the Global Food Crisis, And What They Can do to Stop It," policy briefing, July 2, 2008.

23. Lorne Matalon, "Mexico's Poor Seek Relief From Tortilla Shortage," *National Geographic News* June 4, 2008.

24. Sara Miller Llana, "Mexican farmers replace tequila plant with corn," *Christian Science Monitor,* June 21, 2007.

25. *Associated Press*, "Higher Prices for Food are About to Get Worse," March 16, 2011.

26. Elisabeth Rosenthal, "Rush to Use Crops as Fuel Raises Food Prices and Hunger Fears," *New York Times*, April 16, 2011.

27. Energy Information Administration, "2009 Ethanol Production Exceeds 10.7 Billion Gallons," Renewable Fuels Association, February 26, 2010.

28. Organisation for Economic Co-operation and Development and Food and Agriculture Organization of the United Nations, "Agricultural Outlook 2011-2020," 2011.

29. Caroline Henshaw, "Land for Biofuels or Crops? The Debate Rumbles on," *Wallstreet Journal* June 22, 2011.

30. US Bureau of the Census, "Statistical Abstract of the United States: 2012," 2011.

31. Cheryl J. Trench, "Oil Market Basics: A primer on oil markets combined with hotlinks to oil price and volume data available on the Internet," US Energy Information Administration, n.d.

32. U.S. Energy Information Administration, "Brazil: Country Analysis Brief," July 14, 2010, http://www.eia.gov/countries/country-data.cfm?fips=BR (accessed November 7, 2011).

9: ENERGY ALTERNATIVES

1. *Readers Digest*, Off the Beaten Path, 2003.

2. U2, *The Joshua Tree*, 1999.

3. Dictionary.com, "desert," http://dictionary.reference.com/browse/desert (November 16, 2011).

4. William Targ, *The American West: A Treasury of Stories, Legends, Narratives, Songs and Ballads of Western America* (New York: Kessinger Publishing, LLC, 2005).

5. Tye W. Parzybok, *Weather extremes in the West* (Mountain Press, 2004).

6. Mark Edwin Miller, *Forgotten Tribes: Unrecognized Indians and the Federal Acknowledgment Process* (Lincoln, Nebraska: University of Nebraska Press, 2006).

7. Philip W. Rundel and Arthur C. Gibson, Ecological Communities and Processes in a Mojave Desert Ecosystem (Great Britain: Cambridge University Press, 2005).

8. BrightSource, "BrightSource Projects: IVANPAH," http://www.brightsourceenergy.com/projects/ivanpah (accessed October 11, 2010).

9. Ibid.

10. Dana Hull, "Clean energy 'gold rush' in Mojave spurs backlash," *Christian Science Monitor*, October 31, 2011, http://www.csmonitor.com/Innovation/2011/1031/Clean-energy-gold-rush-in-Mojave-spurs-backlash.

11. Jimmy Carter, "Proposed Energy Policy," *Vital Speeches of the Day*, May 1 1977: 418-420.

12. Los Angeles Department of Power and Water, "Los Angeles Solar Energy Plan," 2008.

13. Lewis Smith, "Solar panels in the Sahara 'could power the whole of Europe'," *The Times*, March 12, 2009.

14. Jonathan Parkinson, "The Not-So-Sunny Side of Solar Panels," February 15, 2009, Voice of San Diego http://www.voiceofsandiego.org/science/article_37811382-9d69-5936-adeb-5db1395225e3.html (accessed November 11, 2011).

15. Daniel Wartenberg, Daniel Reyner and Cheryl Siegel, "Trichloroethylene and Cancer: Epidemiologic Evidence," *Environmental Health Perspectives*, May 2000, Suppl 2:161-76.

16. Ariana Eunjung Cha, "Solar Energy Firms Leave Waste Behind in China," *Washington Post*, March 9, 2008.

17. Hull, "Clean energy 'gold rush' in Mojave spurs backlash."

18. Todd Woody, "Nevada's solar building boom," *Reuters*, November 29, 2010.

19. Todd Woody. "Alternative Energy Projects Stumble on a Need for

Water," *New York Times*, September 29, 2009.

20. Michael Grunwald, "America's Untapped Energy Resource: Boosting Efficiency," *Time*, December 31, 2008, http://www.time.com/time/magazine/article/0,9171,1869224,00.html.

21. *BBC News*, "Rum remark wins Rumsfeld an award," December 2, 2003, http:/news.bbc.co.uk/2/hi/3254852.stm> (accessed November 29, 2011)

22. *Associated Press*, "Texas wetland restoration could be model for Gulf," July 1, 2011.

23. Philip M. Fearnside, "Do Hydroelectric Dams Mitigate Global Warming? The Case of Brazils Curua-Una Dam," *Mitigation and Adaptation Strategies for Climate Change* 10, no. 4 (October 2005): 675-691.

24. Ibid.

25. International Council for the Exploration of the Sea, "Environmental Interactions of Wave and Tidal Energy Generation Devices," Report of the ICES Advisory Committee, 2010.

26. US Department of Energy,"Clean Power Generation—Market and Policy Drivers," http://seca.doe.gov/KeyIssues/clean_power2.html (accessed November 29, 2011).

27. Tad W. Patzek and David Pimentel, "Thermodynamics of Energy Production from Biomass," *Critical Reviews in Plant Sciences* 24 (2005): 327-364.

28. European Renewable Energy Council, "energy [r]evolution: A Sustainable Global Energy Outlook," January 2007.

29. Grunwald, "America's Untapped Energy Resource: Boosting Efficiency."

30. Renewable Fuels Association, "2009 Ethanol Production Exceeds 10.7 Billion Gallons," http://www.ethanolrfa.org/news/entry/2009-ethanol-production-exceeds-10.7-billion-gallons/ (accessed November 11, 2011).

31. World Economic Forum, "Energy Vision Update 2010: Towards a More Energy Efficient World," 2010.

32. Leora Broydo Vestel, "Consumers Buy More Efficient Refrigerators, but Keep the Old Ones Humming," *New York Times Green Blog*, March 19, 2010, http://green.blogs.nytimes.com/2010/03/19/consumers-buy-more-efficient-refrigerators-but-keep-the-old-ones-humming/ (accessed July 1, 2011).

33. Stan Cox, *Losing Our Cool: Uncomfortable Truths About Our Air-Conditioned World (and Finding New Ways to Get Through the Summer)* (New York: The New Press, 2010).

34. Jukka Heinonen and Seppo Junnila, "Implications of urban structure on carbon consumption in metropolitan areas," *Environmental Research Letters*, March 28, 2011.

10: OUR CONSUMPTION PROBLEM

1. Stephanie Zacharek, "IKEA is as bad as Wal-Mart," July 12, 2009, *Salon.com*, http://www.salon.com/2009/07/12/cheap/ (December 2, 2011).

2. Paul Hawken, Armory Lovins and L. Hunter Lovins, *Natural Capitalism: Creating the Next Industrial Revolution* (New York: Back Bay Books, 2008).

3. Jukka Heinonen and Seppo Junnila, "Implications of urban structure on carbon consumption in metropolitan areas," *Environmental Research Letters*, March 28, 2011.

4. Self Storage Association, "Self Storage Association Fact Sheet," http://www.selfstorage.org/ssa/Content/NavigationMenu/AboutSSA/FactSheet/default.htm (accessed on November 29, 2011).

5. Nicole Pasulka, "Running the Numbers," *The Morning News*, July 23, 2007 http://www.themorningnews.org/gallery/running-the-numbers (accessed December 3, 2011).

6. US Environmental Protection Agency, "Municipal Solid Waste Generation, Recycling, and Disposal in the United States: Facts and Figures for 2008," 2009.

7. World Resources Institute, the United Nations Environment Programme, the United Nations Development Programme, and The World Bank, "World Resources 1998-99: Environmental change and human health," 1998.

8. Nielsen Wire, "U.S. Homes Add Even More TV Sets in 2010," April 28, 2010, http://blog.nielsen.com/nielsenwire/consumer/u-s-homes-add-even-more-tv-sets-in-2010/ (accessed December 3, 2011).

9. U.S. Environmental Protection Agency: Office of Solid Waste, "Electronics Waste Management in the United States: EPA530-R-08-009," report, July 2008.

10. M.L. Socolof, et., "Life-cycle environmental impacts of CRT and LCD desktop monitors," *Electronics and the Environment*, Proceedings of the 2001 IEEE International Symposium, 2001: 119-127 .

11. Peter Ostendorp, Suzanne Foster and Chris Calwell, "Televisions: Active Mode Energy Use and Opportunities for Energy Savings," issues paper, Natural Resources Defense Council, March 2005.

12. Bureau of Labor Statistics, "Purchasing Goods and Services," .American Time Use Survey, June 22, 2011, http://www.bls.gov/tus/current/purchasing.htm (December 3, 2011).

11: CRASH THE SYSTEM OR TRASH THE PLANET

1. Jon Herskovitz, "The world is getting hotter, with 2011 one of the warmest years on record, and humans are to blame, a report by the World Meteorological Organization (WMO) said on Tuesday," *Reuters*, November 30, 2011, http://www.reuters.com/article/2011/11/30/us-climate-conference-idUSTRE7AS0MQ20111130 (accessed December 3, 2011).

2. ecoAmerica and SRI Consulting,"The American Environmental Values Survey: Research Summary" October 2006.

3. US Energy Information Administration, "US Carbon Dioxide Emissions from Energy Sources 2008 Flash Estimate," May 2009, http://www.eia.gov/oiaf/1605/flash/flash.html (accessed December 8, 2011).

4. Ibid.

5. Ibid.

6. Ibid.

7. James Manyika, et al., "Growth and renewal in the United States Retooling America's Economic Engine," McKinsey Global Institute, 2011.

8. *The Economist*, "To lose one decade may be misfortune...Twenty years on Japan is still paying its bubble-era bills," December 2009.

9. Paul Krugman and Robin Wells, *Economics* (New York: Worth Publishers, 2009).

10. Ibid.

11. US Bureau of the Census, "Income, Poverty, and Health Insurance Coverage in the United States: 2010," September 2011.

12. Alisha Coleman-Jensen, et al., "Household Food Security in the United States in 2010," US Department of Agriculture Economic Research Service, September 2011, http://www.ers.usda.gov/Publications/err125/ (accessed December 9, 2011).

13. Ibid.

14. Diana Olick, "Nearly 11 Percent of US Houses Empty," January 31, 2011, *CNBC* http://www.cnbc.com/id/41355854/Nearly_11_Percent_of_US_Houses_Empty (accessed December 9, 2011).

15. Emmanuel Saez and Thomas Piketty, "Income Inequality in the

United States, 1913-1998," *Quarterly Journal of Economics* 2003: 1-39.

16. Dave Gilson and Carolyn Perot, "It's the Inequality, Stupid," *MotherJones*, April/May 2011.

17. Central Intelligence Agency, "Country Comparison: Distribution of Family Income—Gini Index," World Factbook, https://www.cia.gov/library/publications/the-world-factbook/rankorder/2172rank.html (accessed December 10, 2011).

18. Arthur Okun, *Equality and Efficiency: The Big Tradeoff* (Washington D.C:. The Brookings Institution, 1975).

19. Editorial, *Scientific American*, "Safety First, Fracking Second," October 19, 2011 http://www.scientificamerican.com/article.cfm?id=safety-first-fracking-second

20. Organization for Economic Co-operation and Development, "Economic Policy Reforms Going for Growth: A Family Affair: Intergenerational Social Mobility across OECD Countries," 2010 http://www.oecd.org/dataoecd/2/7/45002641.pdf (accessed December 10, 2011).

21. Gregory Acs and Seth Zimmerman, "U.S. intragenerational Economic Mobility From 1984 to 2004: Trends and Implications," Economic Mobility Project: Pew Charitable Trusts, 2008.

22. Ibid.

23. Steve Connor, "Warning: Oil supplies are running out fast," August 3, 2009, *The Independent*, http://www.independent.co.uk/news/science/warning-oil-supplies-are-running-out-fast-1766585.html (December 11, 2011).

24. Alex Renton,"How the world's oceans are running out of fish," *Guardian*, May 10, 2008.

25. Andrew Nusca, "Why we're running out of water," *Smart Planet*, October 27, 2010, http://www.smartplanet.com/blog/smart-takes/why-were-running-out-of-water/11164 (December 8, 2011).

26. The New Encyclopædia Britannica v 4. 2007.

27. Herman Daly, *For The Common Good: Redirecting the Economy toward Community, the Environment, and a Sustainable Future* (Boston: Beacon Press, 1994).

28. US Environmental Protection Agency, "The Life Cycle of a Cell Phone," http://www.epa.gov/osw/education/pdfs/life-cell.pdf (December 9, 2011).

29. Center for the Advancement of the Steady State Economy, "What Is a Steady State Economy?" http://steadystate.org/wp-content/uploads/CASSE_Brief_SSE.pdf (accessed April 15, 2011).

30. Carolyn Merchant, *Radical Ecology: The Search for a Livable World* (New York: Routledge, 2005).

31. Mark Anielski, *The Economics of Happiness: Building Genuine Wealth* (Gabriola Island, British Columbia: New Society Publishers, 2007).

32. Thurston Clarke, *The Last Campaign: Robert F. Kennedy and 82 Days That Inspired America* (New York: Holt Paperbacks, 2009).

33. Robert Putnam, *Bowling Alone* (New York: Touchstone Books by Simon and Schuster, 2001(.

34. Yvon Chouinard and Nora Gallagher, "Don't Buy This Shirt Unless You Need It, " Patagonia: Environmental Essay, 2004, http://www.patagonia.com/us/patagonia.go?asseto id=2388 (accessed December 10, 2011).

35. Saamah Abdallah, et al., *The Happy Planet Index 2.0* (London: The New Economics Foundation, 2009).

36. Interview with author.

12: THE HAPPINESS ECONOMY

1. Orville Schell, "Gross National Happiness," *Red Herring,* January 15, 2002.

2. Nadia Mustafa, "What About Gross National Happiness?" *Time* January 10, 2005.

3. Richard A. Easterlin, "Does Economic Growth Improve the Human Lot?" in *Nations and Households in Economic Growth: Essays in Honor of Moses Abramovitz*, eds. Paul A. David and Melvin W. Reder, (New York: Academic Press, Inc., 1974).

4. Betsey Stevenson and Justin Wolfeder, "Happiness Inequality in the United States," *Journal of Legal Studies* 37 (2008): S33-S79.

5. Kumaravel Rajakumar MD, et al, "Solar Ultraviolet Radiation and Vitamin D A Historical Perspective," *American Journal of Public Health* (October 2007): 1746–1754.

6. Putnam, *Bowling Alone.*

7. John Muir and Scot Miller, *My First Summer in the Sierra* (New York: Houghton Mifflin Harcourt, 2011).

8. Schell, "Gross National Happiness."

9. Derrick Jensen, "Beyond Hope," *Orion* May/June 2006.

10. *The Economics of Happiness*, DVD, directed by Helena Norberg-Hodge, Steven Gorelick, and John Page (2011; Berkely, CA: International Society for Ecology and Culture).

11. Sean Richey, "Manufacturing Trust: Community Currencies and the Creation of Social Capital," *Political Behavior* 21 (February 2007): 69-88.

12. Transition Network, "What is a Transition Initiative?" http://www.transitionnetwork.org/support/what-transition-initiative (accessed December 12, 2011).

13. "Slow Money, "About Slow Money," http://www.slowmoney.org/about (accessed December 10, 2011).

14. Slow Food USA.,"What is Slow Food," http://www.slowfoodusa.org/index.php/slow_food/ (accessed December 10, 2011).

15. Richard Erdoes and John Fire Lame Dee, *Lame Deer: Seeker of Visions* (New York: Simon & Schuster, 2001).

16. John R. Cook, *The Border and the Buffalo: An Untold Story of Southwest Plains: A Story of Mountain and Plain* (Buffalo Gap, Texas: State House Press, 1989).

17. Herman Daly, "Modernizing Henry George," The Daly News, http://steadystate.org/modernizing-henry-george/ (accessed December 11, 2011).

18. Jonah Lehrer, "How the City Hurts Your Brain," *Boston Globe*, January 2, 2009.

19. Qing Li, "Effect of forest bathing trips on human immune function," *Environmental Health and Preventive Medicine*, January 2010: 9-17.

20. Joan Maloof, *Teaching the Trees: Lessons from the Forest (*Athens, GA: University of Georgia Press, 2007).

21. *The Economics of Happiness*, DVD.